THE AMATEUR SPIRIT

The Amateur Spirit

By Bliss Perry

Essay Index Reprint Series

BOOKS FOR LIBRARIES PRESS
FREEPORT, NEW YORK

First Published 1904
Reprinted 1969

STANDARD BOOK NUMBER:
8369-1102-4

LIBRARY OF CONGRESS CATALOG CARD NUMBER:
70-84332

PRINTED IN THE UNITED STATES OF AMERICA

To
A. B. P.

PREFACE

THE half dozen essays that are printed in this volume have sufficient unity, I hope, to justify their publication as a book. The emotions of the author who discovers that he has produced a treatise when he intended only a series of essays may be likened to the surprise of the child who observes that his blocks, piled almost at random, make something that looks like a castle after all. My castle is indeed but a modest one. Yet the essays which make up this volume have all been written, I find, with some reference to the central theme: namely, the significance of the amateur spirit in carrying forward the daily work of our modern world. I have endeavored to illustrate from many fields — from sports and politics, from science and letters — the possibility of combining the professional's skill with the zest and enthusiasm of the amateur.

The first essay is devoted to that general theme. The study of Indifferentism approaches the subject from another side, and one not less fascinating to the observer of human life. The two papers about the College Professor have been chosen, partly because that profession is but little understood by the general public, and partly because it frequently affords a very perfect illustration of the union of an ardent human spirit with a consummate technical expertness. The story of an episode in Nathaniel Hawthorne's spiritual development contributes something, I think, to the understanding of the fusion of normal human interests and sympathies with the purely artistic passion of the born writer. The amateur and the professional in Hawthorne — using both words in their best sense — may be observed with singular clearness in that critical summer of 1838.

An honored and friendly Doctor of Divinity has accused me of endeavoring, in the essay upon Fishing with a Worm, to write allegory. That shall be as the reader chooses to interpret it; but I have certainly tried to picture from the material offered by a favorite pastime, some of the warring motives in the old struggle between the generous and the sordid ways of looking at the world.

PREFACE

I should add that the essay on The Life of a College Professor originally appeared in *Scribner's Magazine*. The others have been printed in *The Atlantic Monthly*.

B. P.

CAMBRIDGE, 1904.

CONTENTS

	PAGE
The Amateur Spirit	1
Indifferentism	35
The Life of a College Professor	67
College Professors and the Public	93
Hawthorne at North Adams	117
Fishing with a Worm	141

THE AMATEUR SPIRIT

THE AMATEUR SPIRIT

ONE interesting result of the British struggle in South Africa was a revival among Englishmen of the spirit of self-examination. The unexpected duration and the staggering cost of the war brought sharply home to them a realization of national shortcomings. When every allowance was made for the natural difficulties against which the British troops so gallantly contended, there remained a good deal of incontrovertible and unwelcome evidence of defective preparation, of inadequate training. The War Office maps were incomplete; the Boer positions were ill reconnoitred; British officers of long experience were again and again outgeneraled by farmers. Of the many frank and manly endeavors to analyze the causes of such a surprising weakness, one of the most suggestive was made by the Hon. George C. Brodrick, Warden of Merton College. In an article published in 1900 he inquired whether his countrymen may well be called, not, as formerly, "a nation of shopkeepers," but, with more justice, a nation of amateurs. "Conspicuous as are the virtues of British soldiers and British officers," he remarks, "these virtues are essentially the virtues of the amateur, and not of the professional, arising from the native vigor of our national temperament, and not from intelligent education or training." [1]

The distinction here made between the amateur and the professional is one that, for ordinary purposes, is obvious enough. The amateur, we are accustomed to say, works for love, and not for money. He cultivates an art or a sport, a study or an employment, because of his taste for it; he is attached to it, not because it gives him a living, but because it ministers to his life. Mr. Joseph Jefferson, for instance, is classed as a professional actor and an amateur painter. Charles Dickens was an amateur actor and a professional novelist. Your intermittent political reformer is an amateur. His opponent, the "ward man," is a professional; politics being both his life and his living, his art and his constant industry.

[1] *The Nineteenth Century*, October, 1900.

In any particular art or sport, it is often difficult to draw a hard-and-fast line between amateur and professional activity. The amateur athlete may be so wholly in earnest as to take risks and to endure hardships which no amount of money would tempt him to undergo. This earnestness has seldom, if ever, been carried so far as it is in our American athletic contests of the present day. Here, for instance, is the testimony of one of the members of the Oxford-Cambridge Golfing Society's team, which won so many victories on the American links in the summer of 1903:

"Apart from the American phraseology and such minor distinctions, golf as played across the Atlantic is fundamentally different from the English, and more especially the Scotch variety of the game. At bottom the game in America is a business. At bottom the game in England is a pleasure, a relaxation, and a means of taking pleasant exercise. No doubt from its enthralling nature golf in England has devotees to whom the game is a 'pleasure that's all but pain,' but even so, the attitude of this minority is different from the great bulk of American players who have set golf upon such a pedestal that it has dominated them as a 'pain that is almost a pleasure.' . . .

"The whole attitude towards golf is one of comparison, just as in other branches of life. The American is intensely interested in the tallest building, the richest man, the longest street, the fastest train, and a host of other such combinations which sound like exercises out of an elementary German grammar. It is imagined that there is a list, at the head of which is the best player, with the rest below him in descending scale of efficiency. . . .

"The title of champion does not carry with it honor and congratulation, but rather liability to attack and disparagement if the holder does not win every single match or competition in which he plays. This criticism may be important from the business point of view of the professional, as an advertisement, but it cannot possibly affect an amateur who has nothing whatever to gain or lose pecuniarily by being champion. The principle is to put a man at the head of a list and then tear him down by all available means. . . . This continual golf-playing with an object does away with the light-hearted and cheery matches and foursomes which are the main part of golf in the United Kingdom. The game under this treatment easily loses its title to be called a game, and becomes a serious proposition, blighted with responsibilities and overburdened with care. There is no relaxation in golf of this kind, but only increased consumption of both physical and mental energy." [1]

And here is a Harvard rowing-man writing with admirable frankness in a recent number of *The Harvard Graduates' Magazine,* under the title " Sport or Business ": " I have known but one 'Varsity athlete (I refer particularly to football and rowing as the most strenuous branches of our sport) who admitted for a moment that he went out for the fun he got from the practice and the contest. . . .

" As the thing now stands a man may have the best of personal reasons for not playing, but if he is a good athlete his duty to the college demands a sacrifice of these. The duty to get Yale beaten is just now reckoned to be the athlete's sole duty, while his duty to his present and future self looms small in the background, or vaguely in the

[1] J. A. T. Bramston in *Golf.*

middle distance. It is hard lines for men who are unable to adapt themselves to such a perspective, and who are made to feel ashamed of this as of a weakness. They bear indeed the 'athlete's burden.' And there are too many such men, — men who thoroughly dislike their work under the present extreme conditions, moral as well as physical, and who do it only from a vague feeling that it is 'up to them' to stake their persons in the general obligation to organize victory.

"The spirit that makes a man, when he has once undertaken a thing, put it through to a finish and win out no matter what it costs (and this was once given as a definition of the Yale spirit), is an excellent maxim for business or politics, and one that is frequently heard in defense of the present teeth-gritting state of affairs between Harvard and Yale. But such a maxim cannot be applied to athletics. It means the death of athletics. Its place is in the prize-ring or anywhere you please save in a branch of activity which is essentially a recreation. The true amateur athlete, the true sportsman, is one who takes up sport for the fun of it and the love of it, and to whom success or defeat is a secondary matter so long as the play is good. .... Rivalry is a vital element of sport; it is from doing the thing well, doing the thing handsomely, doing the thing intelligently that one derives the *pleasure* which is the essence of sport. Even more vital than the rivalry itself is the checking of its fierceness and bitterness by the graciousness of gentlemanly feeling. It must be remembered that pure rivalry is fighting, and the more its part is magnified in sport the more sport takes on the nature of a fight, — the nature of the sport which has come to exist between Harvard and Yale. We have to admit that there are some of us who prefer fighting-fun to sport, and there is no doubt that the fighting is a healthy discipline; but the majority of us do not, and there is no reason why our athletics should be moulded to suit the taste of the former, — that we should be made to take our fun with all these convulsions and hysterics. Yet just as long as we meet the present-day Yale such will be the state of things. . . .

"I am well aware of the construction which a part of the public would put upon Harvard's giving up contests with Yale. 'Hopeless of victory,' it would be repeated, 'and like a sulky child, she won't play!' To make my own meaning clear let me repeat that not the loss of victories, but fear of the loss of the true amateur spirit here would be what would urge Harvard to such a course. I have rowed against Yale three times, twice in minor crews which beat her, and once in a university boat which she beat handsomely. I should be willing to see her beat Harvard incessantly if the business and hysterical elements of the thing could be left out. And for these elements it is by no means fair to blame Yale exclusively, though her 'spirit' is popularly understood to include them. The contestants if left to themselves would not develop this spirit to such excess. It comes from outside pressure, from the papers, the graduates, the non-athletic undergraduates, the crowd of betting toughs who turn up at every important game, and, in general, the false 'friends of sport.' "[1]

The athletic contests of zealous undergraduates are of course but one illustration of the earnestness which the amateur may carry into every department of life. Amateur philanthropy, for

[1] William James, Jr., in *The Harvard Graduates' Magazine*, December, 1903.

example, is of great and increasing service in the social organism of the modern community. Many an American brings to his amusement, his avocation, — such as yachting, fancy farming, tarpon fishing, — the same thoroughness, energy, and practical skill that win him success in his vocation.

And yet, as a general rule, the amateur betrays amateurish qualities. He is unskillful because untrained; desultory because incessant devotion to his hobby is both unnecessary and wearisome; ineffective because, after all, it is not a vital matter whether he succeed or fail. The amateur actor is usually interesting, at times delightful, and even, as in the case of Dickens, powerful; his performance gives pleasure to his friends; but, nevertheless, the professional, who must act well or starve, acts very much better. In a country where there is a great leisure class, as the Warden of Merton points out, amateurism is sure to flourish. "The young Englishman of this great leisure class," he says, "is no dandy and no coward, but he is an amateur born and bred, with an amateur's lack of training, an amateur's contempt of method, and an amateur's ideal of life." The English boy attends school, he adds, with other boys who are amateurs in their studies, and almost professionals in their games; he passes through the university with the minimum of industry; he finds professional and public life in Great Britain crippled by the amateur spirit; in the army, the bar, the church, in agriculture, manufacturing, and commerce, there is a contempt for knowledge, an inveterate faith in the superiority of the rule of thumb, a tendency to hold one's self a little above one's work.

Similar testimony has also been given by Mandell Creighton, the late Bishop of London, in a posthumously published address entitled " A Plea for Knowledge." " The great defect of England at present," confesses the bishop, " is an inadequate conception of the value of knowledge in itself, and of its importance for the national life. We have a tendency to repose on our laurels; to adopt the attitude that we are no longer professionals, but high-minded and eclectic amateurs. . . . We do not care to sacrifice our dignity by taking undue care about trifles." [1]

With the validity of such indictments against

[1] *Contemporary Review*, April, 1901.

a whole nation we have no direct concern. But they suggest the importance of the distinction between the amateur and the professional spirit. They show that a realization of this distinction may affect many phases of activity, personal and national. They indicate how far reaching may be its significance for us Americans as we face those new conditions under which the problems of both personal and national life must be worked out.

Amateurs, then, to borrow Mr. Brodrick's definition, "are men who are not braced up to a high standard of effort and proficiency by a knowledge that failure may involve ruin, who seldom fully realize the difficulties of success against trained competitors, and who therefore rebel against the drudgery of professional drill and methodical instruction." One may accept this definition, in all its implications, without ceasing to be aware of the charm of the amateur. For the amateur surely has his charm, and he has his virtues, — virtues that have nowhere wrought more happily for him than here upon American soil. Versatility, enthusiasm, freshness of spirit, initiative, a fine recklessness of tradition and precedent, a faculty for cutting across lots, — these are the qualities of the American pioneer. Not in the Italians of the Renaissance nor in the Elizabethan Englishmen will one find more plasticity of mind and hand than among the plain Americans of 1840. Take those men of the Transcendentalist epoch, whose individuality has been fortunately transmitted to us through our literature. They were in love with life, enraptured of its opportunities and possibilities. No matter to what task a man set his hand, he could gain a livelihood without loss of self-respect or the respect of the community. Let him try teaching school, Emerson would advise; let him farm it a while, drive a tin peddler's cart for a season or two, keep store, go to Congress, live "the experimental life." Emerson himself could muse upon the oversoul, but he also raised the best Baldwin apples and Bartlett pears in Concord, and got the highest current prices for them in the Boston market. His friend Thoreau supported himself by making sand-paper or lead pencils, by surveying farms, or by hoeing that immortal patch of beans; his true vocation being steadily that of the philosopher, the seeker. The type has been preserved, by the translucent art of Hawthorne, in the person of Holgrave, the daguerreotypist of *The House of the Seven Gables*. Holgrave was twenty-two, but he had already been a schoolmaster, storekeeper, editor, peddler, dentist. He had traveled in Europe, joined a company of Fourierists, and lectured on mesmerism. Yet " amid all these personal vicissitudes," Hawthorne tells us, " he had never lost his identity. He had never violated the innermost man, but had carried his conscience along with him."

No doubt there is something humorous, to our generation, in this glorification of the Yankee tin peddler. Yet how much there is to admire in the vivacity, the resourcefulness, the very mobility, of that type of man, who was always in light marching order, and who, by flank attack and feigned retreat and in every disguise of uniform, stormed his way to some sort of moral victory at last! And the moral victory was often accompanied by material victory as well. These men got on, by hook or by crook; they asked no favors; they paid off their mortgages, and invented machines, and wrote books, and founded new commonwealths. In war and peace they had a knack for getting things done, and learning the rules afterward.

Nor has this restless, inventive, querying, accomplishing type of American manhood lost its prominence in our political and social structure. The self-made man is still, perhaps, our most representative man. Native shrewdness and energy and practical capacity — qualities such as the amateur may possess in a high degree — continue to carry a man very far. They have frequently been attended by such good fortune as to make it easy for us to think that they are the only qualities needed for success. Some of the most substantial gains of American diplomacy, for instance, have been made by men without diplomatic training. We have seen within a very few years an almost unknown lawyer, from an insignificant city, called to be the head of the Department of State, where his achievements, indeed, promptly justified his appointment. The case of Judge Day is by no means unique. The conduct of the War Department and the Navy has frequently been intrusted to civilians whose frank ignorance of their new duties has been equaled only by their skill in performing them. The history of

American cabinets is, in spite of many exceptions, on the whole, an apotheosis of the amateur. It is the readiest justification of the tin peddler theory, — the theory, namely, that you should first get your man, and then let him learn his new trade by practicing it. " By dint of hammering one gets to be a blacksmith," say the French ; and if a blacksmith, why not a postmaster, or a postmaster-general, or an ambassador ?

The difficulty with this theory lies in the temptation to exaggerate it. Because we have been lucky thus far, we are tempted to proceed upon the comfortable conviction that if we once find our man, the question of his previous apprenticeship to his calling, or even that of his training in some related field of activity, may safely be ignored. The gambler is in our blood. We like to watch the performance of an untried man in a responsible position, much as we do the trotting of a green horse. The admitted uncertainty of the result enhances our pleasure in the experiment. In literature, just now, we are witnessing the exploitation of the " young writer." Lack of experience, of craftsmanship, is actually counted among a fledgeling author's assets. The curiosity of the public regarding this new, unknown power is counted upon to offset, and more, the recognition of the known power of the veteran writer. Power is indeed recognized as the ultimate test of merit; but there is a widespread tendency to overlook the fact that power is largely conditioned upon skill, and that skill depends not merely upon natural faculty, but upon knowledge and discipline. The popularity of the " young writer " is, in short, an illustration of the easy glorification of amateur qualities to the neglect of professional qualities.

This tendency is the more curious because of our pronounced national distaste for ineffectiveness. The undisguisedly amateurish traits of unskillfulness and desultoriness have not been popular here. If we have been rather complaisant toward the jack-of-all-trades, we have never wholly forgotten that he is "master of none." In the older New England vernacular, the village ne'er-do-well was commonly spoken of as a " clever " fellow; the adjective was distinctly opprobrious. And indeed, if the connoisseur is the one who knows, and the dilettante the one who only thinks he knows, the amateur is often the one who would like to know, but is too lazy to learn. Accordingly, he keeps guessing, in an easy, careless, "clever" fashion, which is agreeable enough when no serious interests are at stake. He has transient affections for this and that department of thought or activity; like Mr. Brooke in *Middlemarch*, he has "gone into that a good deal at one time." Mr. Brooke is a delightful person in fiction, but in actual life a great many Mr. Brookes end their career at the town farm. Even this would not in itself be so lamentable a matter, if it were not in the power of a community of Mr. Brookes to create conditions capable of driving the rest of us to the town farm. "Dilettanteism, hypothesis, speculation, a kind of amateur search for truth, — this," says Carlyle, "is the sorest sin."

The amateur search for truth has always flourished, and is likely to flourish always, in the United States. That the quest is inspiriting, amusing, sometimes highly rewarded, one may readily admit. But if it promotes individualism, it also produces the crank. If it brevets us all as philosophers, it likewise brands many of us as fools. Who does not know the amateur economist, with his "sacred ratios," or his amiable willingness to "do something for silver"? The amateur sociologist, who grows strangely confused if you ask him to define Sociology? Popular preachers, who can refute Darwin and elucidate Jefferson "while you wait,"— if you do wait? Amateur critics of art and literature, who have plenty of zeal, but no knowledge of standards, no anchorage in principles? The lady amateur, who writes verses without knowing prosody, and paints pictures without learning to draw, and performs what she calls "social service" without training her own children either in manners or religion? Nay, are there not amateur teachers who walk gracefully through the part, but add neither to the domain of human knowledge nor to the practical efficiency of any pupil?

But the roll-call of these dependents and defectives is long enough. The failures of the amateur search for truth are often brilliant failures. Its occasional successes have often been brilliant, too. Yet the real workaday progress, the solid irretraceable advance in any art or profession, has commonly been made by the professional. He sums up in himself both connoisseurship and craftsmanship. He not only knows, but does. Pasteur was a professional, and Helmholtz, and

Huxley. John Marshall was a professional jurist. Mr. John Sargent is a professional painter of portraits, and Mr. Secretary Hay is a professional diplomatist.

If the gifted amateur desires to learn his relative rank when compared with a professional, the way is easy. Let him challenge the professional! Play a match at golf against the dour Scotchman who gives lessons for his daily bread. He will beat you, because he cannot afford not to beat you. Shoot against your guide in the North Woods. You will possibly beat him at a target, but he will hit the deer that you have just missed; you can cast a fly on the lawn much farther than he, but he will take more fish out of the pool. It is his business, your recreation. Some one dear to you is critically ill. It seems cruel to surrender the care of the sick person to a hireling, when you are conscious of boundless love and devotion. But your physician will prefer the trained nurse, because the trained nurse will do what she is told, will keep cool, keep quiet, count the drops accurately, read the thermometer right; because, in short, he can depend upon a professional, and cannot depend upon an amateur.

What is true of the sport, of the art, is even more invariably true in the field of scientific effort. How secure is the course of the *Fachmann*, who by limiting his territory has become lord of it, who has a fund of positive knowledge upon all the knowable portions of it, and has charted, at least, the deepening water where knowledge sheers off into ignorance! It is late in the day to confess the indebtedness of our generation to the scientific method. How tonic and heartening, in days of dull routine, has been the example of those brave German masters to whom our American scholarship owes so much! What industry has been theirs, what confidence in method, what serene indifference to the rivalry of the gifted amateur! I recall the fine scorn with which Bernhard ten Brink, at Strassburg, used to wave aside the suggestions of his pupils that this or that new and widely advertised book might contain some valuable contribution to his department. "Nay," he would retort, "*wissenschaftliche Bedeutung hat's doch nicht.*" Many a pretentious book, a popular book, even a very useful book, was pilloried by that quiet sentence, "*It has no scientific significance.*" To get the import of that sentence thoroughly into one's head is worth all it costs to sit at the feet of German scholars. There speaks the true, patient, scientific spirit, whose service to the modern man was perhaps the most highly appraised factor when we of the western world tried to take an inventory of ourselves and our indebtedness, at the dawn of the twentieth century.

For to be able to assess the scientific bearing of the new book, the new fact, upon your own profession proves you a master of your profession. Modern competitive conditions are making this kind of expert knowledge more and more essential. The success of German manufacturing chemists, for example, is universally acknowledged to be due to the scientific attainments of the thousands of young men who enter the manufactories from the great technical schools. The alarm of Englishmen over the recent strides of Germany in commercial rivalry is due to a dawning recognition of the efficacy of knowledge, and of the training which knowledge recommends. It is the well-grounded alarm of the gifted amateur when compelled to compete with the professional. The professional may not be a wholly agreeable antagonist; he may not happen to be a "clubable" person; but that fact does not vitiate his record. His record stands.

Is it possible to explain this patent or latent antagonism of the amateur toward the professional? It is explicable, in part at least, through a comparison not so much of their methods of work — where the praise must be awarded to the professional — as of their characteristic spirit. And here there is much more to be said for the amateur. The difference will naturally be more striking if we compare the most admirable trait of the amateur spirit with the least admirable trait of the professional spirit.

The cultivated amateur, who touches life on many sides, perceives that the professional is apt to approach life from one side only. It is a commonplace to say that without specialized training and accomplishment the road to most kinds of professional success is closed. Yet, through bending one's energies unremittingly upon a particular task, it often happens that creation narrows "in man's view," instead of widening. Your famous expert, as you suddenly discover, is but a segment of a man, — overdeveloped in one direction, atrophied in all others. His expertness, his professional functioning, so to speak, is of indisputable value to society, but he himself remains an unsocial member of the body politic. He has become a machine, — as Emerson declared so long ago, " a thinker, not a man thinking." He is uninterested, and consequently uninteresting. Very possibly it may not be the chief end of man to afford an interesting spectacle to the observer. And yet so closely are we bound together that a loss of sympathy, of imagination, of free and varied activity, soon insulates the individual, and lessens his usefulness as a member of society. Surely we are playing an interesting comedy, here between heaven and the mire, and we ought to play it in an interested way. We can afford to be human. Scientific Method is a handmaiden whose services have proved indispensable. No one can fill her place. We should raise her wages. But, after all, Personality is the mistress of the house. Method must be taught to know her station, and

"She is the second, not the first."

No doubt there is a temptation, in such a comparison of qualities and gifts, to dally with mere abstractions. None of us have known a wholly methodized, mechanicalized man. But none the less we may properly endeavor to measure a tendency, and to guard against its excess. There are few observers of American life who believe that specialization has as yet been carried too far. Yet one may insist that the theory of specialized functions, necessitated as it is by modern conditions, and increasingly demanded as it must be while our civilization grows in complexity, needs examination and correction in the interests of true human progress. It is not that we actually meet on the sidewalk some scientific Frankenstein, some marvelously developed special faculty for research or invention or money-making, which dominates and dwarfs all other faculties, — though we often see something that looks very much like it. It is rather that thoughtful people are compelled to ask themselves, How far can this special development — this purely professional habit of mind — proceed without injury to the symmetry of character, without impairing the varied and spontaneous and abundant play of human powers which gives joy to life? And the prejudice which the amateur feels toward the professional, the more or less veiled hostility between the man who does something for love which another man does for money, is one of those instinctive reactions — like the vague alarm of some wild creature in the woods — which give a hint of danger.

Let us make the very fullest acknowledgment of our debt to the professional spirit. Many of our best inheritances, such as our body of law, represent the steady achievements of professional skill, professional self-sacrifice. The mechanical conveniences and equipments in which the age abounds, all this apparatus for communication and transportation, have been wrought out for us by the most patient, the most concentrated activity of professionals. The young man who is entering medicine, the law, business, the army, the church, finds himself ranked at once by his power to assimilate the professional experience of older men. Some day, let us trust, the young man who desires to serve his country in her civil service, her consular and diplomatic service, will find himself, not as now, blocked by an amateurish system of rewards for partisan fealty, but upon the road to a genuine professional career. The hope of society, no doubt, depends largely upon those men who are seriously devoting their energies to some form of expert activity. They are the torch-bearers, the trained runners who bear the light from stage to stage of the heaven-beholden course. And at least in the immediate future the necessity for unwearying professional endeavor will be more pressing than ever before in the history of the world.

> " Cities will crowd to its edge
> In a blacker incessanter line;
> . . . The din will be more on its banks,
> Denser the trade on its stream."

Ours must be, not "a nation of amateurs," but a nation of professionals, if it is to hold its own in the coming struggles, — struggles not merely for commercial dominance, but for the supremacy of political and moral ideals. Our period of national isolation, with all it brought of good or evil, has been outlived. The new epoch will place a heavy handicap upon ignorance of the actual world, upon indifference to international usages and undertakings, upon contempt for the foreigner. What is needed is, indeed, knowledge, and the skill that knowledge makes possible. The spirit with which we confront the national tasks of the future should have the sobriety, the firmness, the steady effectiveness, which we associate with the professional.

Yet is it not possible, while thus acknowledging and cultivating the professional virtues, to free ourselves from some of the grosser faults of the mere professional? The mere professional's cupidity, for instance, his low aim, his time-serving, his narrowness, his clannish loyalty to his own department only? How often he lacks imagination! How indifferent he may show himself to the religious and moral passion, to the dreams, hopes, futilities, regrets of the breathing, bleeding, struggling men and women by his side! It is not the prize-fighter only who brings professionalism into disrepute. The jockey who "pulls" a horse, the oarsman who "sells" a race, the bicyclist who fouls a rival, are condemned even by a mob of "sporting men." But the taint of professionalism clings also to the business man who can think only of his shop, the scholar who talks merely of letters, the politician who asks of the proposed measure, "What is there in this for *me?*" To counteract all such provinciality and selfishness, such loss of the love of honor in the love of gain, one may rightly plead for some breath of the spirit of the amateur, the *amator*, the "man who loves;" the man who works for the sheer love of working, plays the great complicated absorbing game of life for the sake of the game, and not for his share of the gate money; the man who is ashamed to win if he cannot win fairly, — nay, who is chivalric enough to grant breathing-space to a rival, whether he win or lose!

Is it an impossible ideal, this combination of qualities, this union of the generous spirit of the amateur with the method of the professional? In the new world of disciplined national endeavor upon which we are entering, why may not the old American characteristics of versatility, spontaneity, adventurousness, still persist? These are the traits that fit one to adjust himself readily to unforeseen conditions, to meet new emergencies. They will be even more valuable in the future than in the past, if they are employed to supplement, rather than to be substituted for, the solid achievements of professional industry. If we are really to lead the world's commerce, — though that is far from being the only kind of leadership to which American history should teach us to aspire, — it will be the Yankee characteristics, plus the scientific training of the modern man, that will enable us to do it. The personal enthusiasm, the individual initiative, the boundless zest, of the American amateur must penetrate, illuminate, idealize, the brute force, the irresistibly on-sweeping mass, of our vast industrial democracy.

The best evidence that this will happen is the fact that it is already happening. There are here and there amateurs without amateurishness, professionals untainted by professionalism. Many of us are fortunate enough to recognize in some friend this combination of qualities, this union of strict professional training with that free outlook upon life, that human curiosity and eagerness, which are the best endowment of the amateur. Such men are indeed rare, but they are prized accordingly. And one need hardly say where they are most likely to be found. It is among the ranks of those who have received a liberal education. Every higher institution of learning in this country now offers some sort of specialized training. To win distinction in academic work is to come under the dominion of exact knowledge, of approved methods. It means that one is disciplined in the mechanical processes and guided by the spirit of modern science, no matter what his particular studies may have been. The graduates whose acquisitions can most readily be assessed are probably the ones who have specialized most closely, who have already as undergraduates begun to fit themselves for some form of professional career. They have already gained something of the expert's solid basis of accurate information, the expert's sureness of hand and eye, the expert's instinct for the right method.

But this professional discipline needs tempering by another spirit. The highest service of the educated man in our democratic society demands of him breadth of interest as well as depth of technical research. It requires unquenched ardor for the best things, spontaneous delight in the play of mind and character, a many-sided responsiveness that shall keep a man from hardening into a mere high-geared machine. It is these qualities that perfect a liberal education and complete a man's usefulness to his generation. Taken by themselves, they fit him primarily for living, rather than for getting a living. But they are not to be divorced from other qualities; and even if they were, the educated American can get a living more easily than he can learn how to live. The moral lessons are harder than the intellectual, and faith and enthusiasm, sympathy and imagination, are moral qualities.

Here, for example, is some young scholar who has been taught the facts of history, trained to sift historical evidence, to compare historical periods, to trace historical causes; but has he imagination enough to see into the mind and heart of the historical man? He has been taught to analyze the various theories of society and government; he has learned to sneer at what he calls "glittering generalities;" yet has he sympathy enough, moral passion enough, to understand what those glittering generalities have done for the men and the generations that have been willing to die for them? Such secrets forever elude the cold heart and the calculating brain. But they are understood by the generous youth, by the man who is brave enough to take chances, to risk all for the sake of gaining all. It is for this reason that the amateur football game, for all its brutalities, has taught many a young scholar a finer lesson than the classroom has taught him, namely, to risk his neck for his college; yet no finer one than the classroom might afford him if his teacher were always an *amator*, — a lover of virility as well as of accuracy; a follower not of the letter only, but of the spirit which makes alive. " Our business in this world," said Robert Louis Stevenson, — a craftsman who through all his heart-breaking professional toil preserved the invincible gayety of the lover, — " is not to succeed, but to continue to fail in good spirits." In this characteristically Stevensonian paradox there is a perfect and a very noble expression of the amateur spirit. He does not mean, we may be sure, that failure is preferable to success, but that more significant than either success or failure is the courage with which one rides into the lists. It is his moral attitude toward his work which lifts the workman above the fatalities of time and chance, so that, whatever fortune befall the labor of his hands, the travail of his soul remains undefeated and secure.

INDIFFERENTISM

INDIFFERENTISM

READERS of books have sometimes debated the question, " What was the greatest book produced during the eighteenth century ? " Was it Goethe's *Faust*, or Jonathan Edwards on the *Freedom of the Will?* Was it Gibbon's *Decline and Fall*, or that romance of Fielding's which Gibbon declared would " outlive the palace of the Escurial, and the imperial eagle of the house of Austria " ?

It is hard to answer such a question, and very likely it is foolish to try. An easier task is to name the wittiest book of that century. One may do so without much fear of contradiction. The wittiest eighteenth-century book, surely, — although Wordsworth does call it, and in *The Excursion* at that, a

> " dull product of a scoffer's pen,"

and Hawthorne once fell asleep over it, — is Voltaire's *Candide*, or Optimism. Written in 1759 to satirize the doctrine that ours is the best of all possible worlds, *Candide* presents, in the form of a swiftly moving story, Voltaire's impression of the world as it really is. He exiles his young hero Candide — "a person of the most unaffected simplicity" — from his native castle in Westphalia, separates him from his beloved mistress Cunegunde, and sends him over Europe and America to seek for her and incidentally to observe our mortal situation. Candide is accompanied by an old philosopher named Martin, who has long served as a bookseller's hack and has lost all illusions. As they pass from one European capital to another, Candide still maintains in spite of every disappointment and misfortune that "there is nevertheless some good in the world."

"Maybe so," says Martin, "but it has escaped my knowledge."

Reasoning thus, they arrive at last at Venice, where they hear much talk about a certain noble Venetian, Signor Pococurante, whose name signifies "The-Man-who-cares-little," and who is said to be a perfectly happy man.

"I should be glad to meet so extraordinary a being," says Martin, and accordingly our travelers pay a visit to the noble Pococurante. They find him dwelling in a palace on the Brenta. Its gardens are elegantly laid out and adorned with statues. The master of the palace is a man of sixty, rich, cultivated, bored. He shows the travelers his collection of paintings, among them some by Raphael. "I have what is called a fine collection," he admits, "but I take no manner of delight in them." He orders a concert for his guests, but confesses that he himself finds the music tiresome. After dinner they repair to the library, where Candide, observing a richly bound Homer, commends the noble Venetian's taste.

"Homer is no favorite of mine," answers Pococurante coolly; "I was made to believe once that I took a pleasure in reading him. . . . I have asked some learned men whether they are not in reality as much tired as myself with reading this poet. Those who spoke ingenuously assured me that he had made them fall asleep, and yet that they could not well avoid giving him a place in their libraries."

The conversation shifts to Virgil, Horace, Cicero; to the Memoirs of the Academy of Sciences, to the drama, to English politics, and finally to Milton; but Signor Pococurante finds in all these subjects little or nothing to praise. Candide the optimist is grieved. He has been taught to respect Homer and is fond of Milton.

"Alas," he whispers to Martin, "I am afraid this man holds our German poets in great contempt."

"There would be no such great harm in that," replies Martin.

"Oh, what a surprising man!" exclaims Candide to himself. "What a prodigious genius is this Pococurante! Nothing can please him."

After finishing their survey of the library, they go down into the garden. Candide politely says something in praise of its beauty.

"It is laid out in bad taste," replies Pococurante; "it is childish and trifling; but I shall have another laid out to-morrow upon a nobler plan."

At last the two travelers take leave of their host. "Well," says Candide to Martin, "I hope you will own that this man *is* the happiest of all mortals, for he is above everything he possesses."

"But do you not see," answers Martin, "that he likewise dislikes everything he possesses? It was an observation of Plato long since that those

INDIFFERENTISM 41

are not the best stomachs that reject, without distinction, all sorts of food."

"True," says Candide, "but still there must certainly be a pleasure in criticising everything, and in perceiving faults where others think they see beauties."

"*That is*," retorts Martin, who generally has the last word, "*there is a pleasure in having no pleasure.*"

Few pages of imaginative literature are more admirably written than these whose bare outlines I have been copying. No group of inquirers concerning the intellectual habits and the moral hopes of mankind is more skillfully composed than that formed by the three men who saunter through the library and garden of this palace upon the Brenta: Candide the puzzled young optimist, old Martin the pessimist, grimly delighted, and Pococurante the indifferentist, with his perfect courtesy, his refreshing frankness, his infinite capacity for being bored. In this last personage, particularly, there is something which touches the fancy, provokes curiosity, and possibly, in spite of all disapprobation of the noble Venetian's faults, invites to a closer acquaintance. One may venture therefore to consider the type of mind which the Venetian senator represents, and to discuss, in their bearing upon the life of the modern man, some of the old and new forms of indifferentism.

For Signor Pococurante is by no means a mere clever invention of Voltaire's. We have met the gentleman before. The type is older than the eighteenth century; older than the Horatian doctrine of *nil admirari;* older even than the Hebrew king who, like the Venetian senator, had his men-singers and women-singers, his banquets and palaces and pleasure-gardens, and grew tired of them all. The weariness of the mind in full possession of its treasures, as that of the body surfeited with its pleasures, is a familiar fact in human history. Pococurantism — the caring little for things that are worth caring much for — lurks deep in human nature. But there are certain conditions that bring the seed of it to full flowering. Every cultivated circle of men and women, every highly organized society, has its Pococurantes; nay, there is some drop of their blood in all of us who have had free access to the fine excitements of the senses, to the wide interests of the mind. Once liberate a man through education and opportunity, once make him a free citizen of the great world of thought, introduce him to affairs, to art and literature, and you give the indifferentism latent in him a chance to develop itself. Is there an educated person who has not noticed among his friends — and, if he be gifted with any power of self-analysis, in himself — this tendency to regard with dissatisfaction, with finical criticism, with satiety, objects which are not only worthy but which once filled him with admiring joy?

Salient examples of this familiar phenomenon are always to be found in communities where the academic type of character is strongly marked. In every university town you will hear much talk of the local Signor Pococurante, some scholar of fastidious temper, of taste scrupulously refined, against whose severe standards of criticism, whether in architecture, poetry, or politics, the heathen rage. How useful such personages often are! Their smiling indifference to the popular verdict strengthens the wavering independence of weaker men. The very irritation produced by their criticism is often proof that the faults they perceive are real faults, and should be remedied. How characteristic of such men is the following passage from the *Memoirs* of Mark Pattison: —

"It is impossible for me to see anything done without an immediate suggestion of how it might be better done. I cannot travel by railway without working out in my mind a better time-table than that in use. On the other hand, this restlessness of the critical faculty has done me good service when turned upon myself. I have never enjoyed any self-satisfaction in anything I have ever done, for I have inevitably made a mental comparison with how it might have been better done. The motto of one of my diaries, 'Quicquid hic operis fiat pœnitet,' may be said to be the motto of my life."

Undoubtedly, this restlessness of the critical faculty contributes to human progress. And how upright may be the character of the super-subtle critic, how singularly attractive his personal charm!

Yet after all, in spite of Candide's ingenuous opinion, the fact that "nothing pleases" a man does not prove him a "prodigious genius." That he is "above everything he possesses" does not demonstrate any native power, any insight of imaginative sympathy. Nor do academic communities present more pathetic figures than the pococurantists who are without fame, influence, or many friends; whose refinement of feeling has degenerated into querulousness, and whose exalted standards of action are chiefly displayed in their ability to coöperate, to any useful purpose, with our American world as it actually is.

No one has yet written, I believe, the History of Academic Sterility. Whoever may do so will consult Gray and Gibbon as to the moral stagnation of the English universities in the eighteenth century, and Mark Pattison as to their intellectual apathy in the middle of the nineteenth. "The men of middle age," says Pattison in speaking of Oxford, "seem, after they reach thirty-five or forty, to be struck with an intellectual palsy, and betake themselves, no longer to port, but to the frippery work of attending boards and negotiating some phantom of legislation, with all the importance of a cabinet council — *belli simulacra cientes*. Then they give each other dinners, where they assemble again with the comfortable assurance that they have earned their evening relaxation by the fatigues of the morning's committee."

But we need not look abroad for such examples of pedantry, of the false air of accomplishment, of arrested development. Fortunate is the American institution that has none of this sterile stock, these men who have been surrounded by books, museums, galleries, only to discover at last that they have no pleasure in them. To describe adequately such types of barrenness one must employ those terrible metaphors used long ago to portray secret causes of spiritual failure. A wins at last his professorship; his desire has been granted, but leanness has been sent into his soul. B possesses all the apparatus of scholarship, but by middle life there is no more oil in his lamp. The lamp goes out, while the man lives on. Yet in the same county, perhaps, there will be men of straitened means, with few modern facilities for research, slender libraries, little converse with fellow scholars, who are nevertheless steadily, quietly, building up a national, an international reputation; while the pococurantist, with everything he needs at his elbow, fairly choked with the riches and pleasures of the scholarly life, not only brings no fruit to perfection, but even fails to produce any fruit at all.

One may be pardoned for thus alluding to the academic type of indifferentism, since its features are so familiar. But there are many varieties of indifferentists, up and down the world, and all of them are worth studying. What sort of man was that Gallio whose unconcern for sectarian controversy has proverbialized him as the man who "cared for none of these things"? I imagine that Gallio was a companionable soul, full of savor, but who knows? And who can tell us authoritatively about the real Horace, that ripe specimen of the genial pococurantist whose bland worldliness, dislike of being bored, and frank indifference to the ambitions and passions of the hour make him such a charming figure? Old Omar Khayyám is a more subtle pococurantist, of the pessimist species; and Edward FitzGerald, Omar's sponsor, was on many sides of his complex personality as perfect a Signor Pococurante as was ever bred by university training and subsequent insulation from the world. Is there not some humanist who will analyze the secret springs of indifferentism in men like these? Is it a defect of the will, or a surplusage of philosophy? Is it a strange torpor of the mind, or is it rather the result of a too keen intelligence? Or is it merely "temperament"? Professor Flint, who has recently dissected Agnosticism with the practiced skill of a Scotch logician, might be asked to make a diagnosis of Pococurantism as well. His book would be interesting reading, but I fancy that Gallio and FitzGerald would put it aside with a quizzical smile.

It is not too fanciful to say that there are indifferentists produced by ignorance, as well as by a surfeit of knowledge. Whole classes and races are apparently doomed to a happy-go-lucky, semi-tropical indolence of body and spirit, — amusing enough to the traveler, but yet dull and blind. It may stretch our Italian word too far, to make it cover these coarser forms of indifference to excellence, — forms that spring from sheer unconsciousness rather than from satiety with the objects of intellectual curiosity. Likewise it may be taking too much liberty with the word to apply it to that unconcern for the ordinary tastes and pleasures of mankind which results from absorption in some supreme issue. How many a mediæval saint demonstrated his sainthood by caring for none of these things that move us to such transports, such pursuits, such struggles! "Did you enjoy the lake?" runs the famous story about St. Bernard, who had been journeying all day beside the waters of Geneva. "Lake?" replied the saint in mild surprise, "what lake?" There may be a strain of ethical nobility, no doubt, in this forgetfulness of all sensuous beauty. But the type of soul represented by the dreaming saint has always been rare, and seems to be growing rarer. Few high-minded men and women are now content to press into the solitary ways of lonely spiritual rapture; the path of progress leads them no longer to cells in the high Alps. The men and women most keenly alive to spiritual issues are insisting upon the social duties, the validity of social instincts, the claims of the innumerable close-woven bonds of human relationship. The true saints, whether of the mediæval or modern type, are never, strictly speaking, Pococurantes. They care infinitely, whether for one or many things, but it is true that their sense of values has been so reversed, as compared with that of ordinary men, that like the risen Lazarus in Browning's poem, the things which seem trivial to us are all important to them, while their great concerns are our trivialities. Yet in this very detachment from the average standard of judgment, in their sense of superiority to their surroundings and possessions, they illustrate, singularly enough, a suggestive phase of indifferentism.

It is evident that I have just been choosing extreme examples. But somewhere between the peasant, who is indifferent to ideas because his eyes are darkened, and the saint, whose inner light makes the world of ideas a mere flickering unreality, stand men like Horace and Horace Walpole, Montaigne and Goethe, Franklin and Jefferson, the speculative, amused, undeluded children of this world. Such men do not lack interest in human affairs, but they weigh all things coolly, and register the gravity or the levity of our mortal predicament with the same smile. Even if no pococurantists themselves, they are the begetters of Pococurantism in others. For behind such representative figures, sharing their recurrent skepticism, but wanting their robust curiosity, their unimpaired sanity, are grouped the great majority of privileged, educated men. Few of them escape some touch, sooner or later, of the temper of indifferentism. With one it is a mere sophomoric affectation, — a pretense of unconcern, — while with another it deepens into lifelong habit. But to all of us at times the mood of "caring little" comes. Subtle are the disguises, puzzling are the contradictory manifestations of the loss of interest in the normally interesting. The child pokes into the inside of its doll, and straightway possesses one delightful mystery the less; the worldling finds his game not worth the candle; the statesman sees his great plans crumbling like a house of cards, and often realizes that at heart he cares for them as little. And all this disillusionment may come, as it did to our Venetian senator, without making the man discourteous or unkind. Indeed it sometimes seems to deepen the pococurantist's humaner qualities, as if disillusionment were the sign of initiation into a world-wide fraternity, the seal of our mortal experience.

Here is a well-known passage from the autobiography of one of the most gentle, honest, and unquestionably great men of our own day. It is the passage where Charles Darwin confesses his loss of interest in certain things which had once moved him deeply. The words are frequently commented upon as illustrating the atrophy of unused faculties. That is indeed their obvious purport, but as you read them, note how perfectly they echo, more than a century afterward, the very tones of Signor Pococurante's confession in his library: —

"I have said that in one respect my mind has changed during the last twenty or thirty years. Up to the age of thirty, or beyond it, poetry of many kinds, such as the works of Milton, Gray, Byron, Wordsworth, Coleridge, and Shelley, gave me great pleasure, and even as a schoolboy I took intense delight in Shakespeare, especially in the historical plays. I have also said that formerly pictures gave me considerable, and music very great delight. But now for many years I cannot endure to read a line of poetry: I have tried lately to read Shakespeare, and found it so intolerably dull that it nauseated me. I have also almost lost my taste for pictures or music. Music generally sets me thinking too energetically on what I have been at work on, instead of giving me pleasure. I retain some taste for fine scenery, but it does not cause me the exquisite delight which it formerly did. . . .

"This curious and lamentable loss of the higher æsthetic tastes is all the odder, as books on history, biographies, and travels (independently of any scientific facts which they may contain), and essays on all sorts of subjects interest me as much as ever they did. My mind seems to have become a kind of machine for grinding general laws out of large collections of facts, but why this should have caused the atrophy of that part of the brain alone, on which the higher tastes depend, I cannot conceive. A man with a mind more highly organized or better constituted than mine would not, I suppose, have thus suffered; and if I had to live my life again, I would have made a rule to read some poetry and listen to some music at least once every week; for perhaps the parts of my brain now atrophied would thus have been kept active through use. The loss of these tastes is a loss of happiness, and may possibly be injurious to the intellect and more probably to the moral character, by enfeebling the emotional part of our nature."

The famous naturalist's experience has been that of countless men whose devotion to their own chosen field has left them more and more oblivious of general human or æsthetic interests. There are plenty of Latinists who read Virgil not for the poetry but for material for a theory of the subjunctive, and they gradually forget that there is any poetry there. It would be easy to multiply examples of this narrowing influence of over-specialization. And it is instructive to note that in every field except the one selected for his concentrated activity, the specialist often offers a curious parallel to his arch-enemy the amateur. Sooner or later, both tend to become pococurantists as regards the majority of subjects of human intercourse. "I went into that a good deal at one time," says Mr. Brooke in *Middlemarch*. It is the typical remark of the typical amateur. "Poetry and pictures formerly gave me great pleasure," says Darwin. "I was once persuaded that I enjoyed Homer and Raphael," says our Venetian senator. The three confessions

INDIFFERENTISM

are identical; the amateur and the specialist have now arrived at the same point as the born pococurantist.

There are other examples of intellectual and moral indifferentism no less striking, although widely different in their source. A jaded American millionaire, trying to get pleasure out of a too long deferred holiday in Europe, is one of the most depressing of pococurantist spectacles. For twenty or thirty years he has been amassing a fortune, with the pluck and energy which we all admire. And here he is set down in Paris or Dresden or Florence, ignorant of the language, the history, the architecture, the ideas of the country. He is a good fellow, but he is homesick, listless, indifferent: he speeds his automobile along some famous Roman road without once kindling at the thought of Cæsar or Napoleon; the Mediterranean means to him Monte Carlo; and nothing in his trip gives him so much real satisfaction as to buttonhole a fellow American and talk to him about the superiority of New York hotels. He is taking his holiday too late. He has no longer any oil in his lamp. Curiosity, imagination, sympathy, zest, have been burned out of him in that fierce competitive struggle where his life forces have been spent. He is a victim of a system, — of the quantitative rather than the qualitative test of excellence. None of our contemporary hallucinations leads more certainly to ultimate weariness and indifferentism than this too exclusive glorification of "men who do things." We worship size, efficiency, tangible results. With the late W. E. Henley in his automobile poem we cry: —

> "Speed —
> Speed, and a world of new havings,
> . . . .
> Learning and Drink
> And Money and Song,
> Ships, Folios, and Horses,
> The craft of the Healer,
> The worship of God
> And things done to the instant
> Delight of the Devil
> And all, all that tends
> To his swift-to-come, swift-to-go
> Glory, are tested,
> Gutted, exhausted,
> Chucked down the draught;
> And the quest, the pursuit,
> The attack, and the conquest

> Of the Unknown goes on —
> *Goes on in the Joy of the Lord.*"

It is a fascinating, record-breaking schedule for the road-race for Success, but a man may without cowardice confess that he is afraid of it. One sees too many broken-down machines in the roadside ditch. Study the faces of the Men Who Do Things, of the Men of To-morrow, as you find them presented in the illustrated periodicals. They are strong, straightforward faces, the sign of a powerful, high-geared bodily mechanism. These men are the winners in the game which our generation has set itself to play. But many of the faces are singularly hard, insensitive, untouched by meditation. If we have purchased speed and power at the cost of nobler qualities, if the men who do things are bred at the expense of the men who think and feel, surely the present American model needs modification.

For there has been a good deal of human history made upon this planet before the invention of the automobile, and one of the most obvious lessons of that history is the moral indifference which is apt to follow upon great material success. We perceive that something is wrong even with the courteous superiority of Signor Pococurante. We feel that it is a flaw in an otherwise kindly and attractive character. But what shall we say of the moral insensibility, the sheer recklessness of human life, the selfish indifference to the welfare of weaker races, in which the present decade abounds? It is a new form of Pococurantism, and one far more dangerous than any dilettante type, because it attacks stronger men.

"Speed, and a world of new havings,"

no matter who or what may lie in the path! That is its watchword. It has taken new accents in our own days, but it is after all the old hoarse shout of Philistinism, trusting in its sword and spear and shield.

Nor are its less militant aspects any less fundamentally barbaric. "How pleasant," says one of the citizens in the Easter Sunday scene in *Faust*, "to sit here and empty your glass and think of the people fighting far away!"

> "On Sundays, holidays, there's naught I take delight in
> Like gossiping of war and war's array,
> Where down in Turkey, far away,
> The foreign people are a-fighting."

But beneath even this softer and more smug Philistinism, — wrapped comfortably in material progress, full of good nature, of benevolent sentiment, of jocosity, — what indifference there may be toward the good old cause of world-wide liberty and fraternity, what essential hardness of heart!

It is a long journey from Venice in the eighteenth century to America in the twentieth. Yet the decaying commercial republic of Italy, drawing to itself even in its decline the treasures of the East and West, offering to the stranger, with a sort of splendid affluence, both its best and its worst, presents more than one likeness to the vast, prosperous America of to-day. Among our countrymen who have enjoyed full opportunities for culture, there are few who have not at times shared the listlessness, the apathy of that Venetian nobleman who was cloyed with his own treasures. How can it be otherwise? How can the man or woman of normal power constantly respond to the multiform stimulus of these swift days of ours? Who can adequately react even to the news contained in the morning paper? Here is the life of the whole world brought daily to the door. But who is ready to weigh it, sift it, assimilate it? No wonder that men and women of fine fibre are conscious too often of that lassitude which comes from wandering through the rooms of a great museum, a weariness like that which oppresses the conscientious sight-seer at a World's Fair.

We cannot rest, meditate, dream, without missing our train, breaking our engagement. We hurry on, through this crowded, absorbing, splendidly rich and varied life of contemporary America, a race of a few athletes and millions of nervous dyspeptics. We are a restless people, hypnotized with transient enthusiasms. To-day we plan a marble archway for a naval hero, build it to-morrow in plaster, and the day after tear it down. We idolize the phrases of the Declaration of Independence for two or three generations, and then suddenly make the discovery that they are mere generalities, good enough for the library, but inapplicable to practical affairs. All the wealth of our physical resources, all the marvels of our tangible success, are not enough, it appears, to save us from the Old World vice of indifferentism, from the swift relapse into disillusionment.

INDIFFERENTISM

Let us come back to Voltaire's parable. He was a master of dialectic weapons, and in this novel about the quest of happiness he scores his point with impeccable precision. Signor Pococurante is not happy. Candide is searching for a perfectly happy person, and he does not find one, even in that admirably furnished palace upon the Brenta. A man's life, in other words, consists not in the abundance of the things which he possesses. Yet the road to happiness is not through caring little, — as the Stoics will still have it, — but through caring much and continuing to care much. It is the ardent, luminous mind, not the smothered, hypercritical mind, which has the truer perception of values. The disillusionized man is not necessarily the wise man. Hamlet was wiser, more truly philosophical in the university at Wittenberg, where he was doubtless taught "What a piece of work is a man! how noble in reason! how infinite in faculty!" than he was later, when, in the stress of unequal conflict with the world, he added the sad personal footnote, "And yet, to me, what is this quintessence of dust?"

In actual human intercourse, furthermore,

your disillusionized man or woman is, to put it plainly, apt to prove himself a bore. It is amusing enough for a while to hear some melancholy Jaques wittily rail and sneer, but it soon grows tiresome. The most agreeable companion in the game of life is what golfers call the "cheerful duffer," who plays shockingly, it is true, but who is always hoping and struggling to beat bogey on the next hole. It is in the mood of the awkward idealist, and not of the graceful pococurantist, that most of the good work of the world is done.

There is plentiful absurdity, no doubt, in the popular interpretation of what has been so widely heralded as the doctrine of "strenuousness." As a counter-gospel to that of mere fault-finding inertia or obstructionism, strenuousness is well enough. But superficially understood, it may mean nothing more than the cult of activity for its own sake; "hustling," as we love to say, for the mere end of being a "hustler." No nation ever needed such a doctrine less than we. We have already too much headlong hurry that does not count: like the nervous pulling on and off of sweaters by the substitutes on the sidelines of a football-field, it shows feverish activity and energy, but it does not advance the ball. The real purport of the strenuous doctrine is rather this: that life is infinitely significant; that it should not be frittered away, either in finical criticism or in foolish, irrelevant activities. It is meant to be used, — intelligently, fully, generously. Those are fine lines of Henry van Dyke: —

> " Life is an arrow — therefore you must know
> What mark to aim at, how to use the bow —
> Then draw it to the head, and let it go ! "

It is the good fortune of some men and women to feel instinctively this potential value of human life. Others learn it tardily, after the oil in the lamp is low. But nothing is more inspiring than to see human beings make the great acceptance, and devote themselves to some generous service. The bow is meant to shoot with, and not to hang on the wall. It improves with age, and so should men and women. " We grow simpler," wrote Thackeray, " as we grow older."

For, after all, these contemporary forms of indifferentism are not final. We shall doubtless specialize more, rather than less, and yet the narrowing tendencies of absorption in one's own specialty may be resisted. The lassitude that marks the reaction from great and long-continued effort is perhaps inevitable; but in those hours one may refresh himself from the deep fountains that spring up within the soul. One's individual success or happiness may tempt him to regard the less fortunate with an indifferent eye, but in a democracy like ours Dives and Lazarus may always be trusted to shift places, if you will but give them time.

To avoid that cold, paralyzing touch of indifferentism, one can at least endeavor to live simply. There is even now apparent, in the press, in many strange pulpits, and in the private talk of men in every section of the country, a wholesome tendency to praise this "simple life." It is perhaps a by-product of prosperity, for the doctrine it praises is more easily followed by the rich than by the poor. A fine simplicity of mind often accompanies great wealth, while poverty is as often the cause of perpetual duplicity and fear. But fortunately for our generation, both rich and poor have been rediscovering Nature. We have found sources of joy in familiar surroundings and in common things. It is one step toward rediscovering ourselves. "Simplification," as Mr. John Morley has so often pointed out, was the motto of that Revolution which followed so swiftly upon the mood of Voltairean doubt; and now that a whole cycle of experience has been accomplished, simplification should be the watchword once more. "Plain living and high thinking" is a hackneyed phrase, and represents for many of us but a forced virtue; yet plain living and high thinking are at least not the soil in which Pococurantism flourishes. A quiet mind that recalls the enduring lessons of history, a meditative mind that perceives the secret of vitality in true books and true men, a sane mind that sees life wholesomely and humanly, — this is what one must cultivate if he would share the inexhaustible freshness, the unceasing energy, which make the daily gladness of the world.

And the last words of Signor Pococurante himself are not to be forgotten. They relate, it may be remembered, to his garden. He is indeed dissatisfied with it, as with everything else, and yet he adds, in words that almost redeem his character and testify to his essentially human quality: "I shall have another laid out to-morrow upon a nobler plan." How persistent, how indestructible is idealism, even in the breast of a professed indifferentist! This idealism is an integral part of our inheritance. Though baffled at every point, it underlies and corrects our transient fits of despondent criticism. Indifferentism should be studied, controlled, counteracted; but in most of us, after all, it is a mood only. It is a shadow on the landscape. Yet far below it in our nature there is the undefeated desire, the imperishable aspiration, that to-morrow may find us dwelling in another garden, built upon a nobler plan. That is our human heritage of toil and hope, and it is a man's part to reënter it daily with courage and good cheer.

THE LIFE OF A COLLEGE
PROFESSOR

THE LIFE OF A COLLEGE PROFESSOR

It is an impertinence to ask a man still in the game whether the game be worth the candle. He thought so once, no doubt, or he would not have begun playing; and the courteous presumption is that he persists in his opinion. Whatever may be his secret guesses as to the value of the stake, your true sportsman will play the game out, and as long as he is playing his best, he makes but an indifferent philosopher. No man absorbed in a profession can assess critically that profession's claims and its rewards, but he can at least recall some of his anticipations upon entering it, and compare them with the realities of his actual experience.

To a young man with some taste for the things of the mind, the life of a college professor offers manifold points of attraction. The candidates for the profession have usually won some distinction as undergraduates, so that from the first moment of post-graduate study one has the feeling of association and rivalry with picked men. The days when the valedictorian was invariably called back to his Alma Mater as a tutor, to be used in any department happening to be short of tutors that year, or when the Rev. Mr. Blinker of Mudville, famous in college as a mighty handler of the lexicon, but quite unappreciated in Mudville, was on that account tolerably sure of getting a professorship, are indeed rapidly receding. Sometimes men drift into college work from other callings, or are drafted from among the teachers in preparatory schools, but the conventional road to promotion is some form of specialized graduate study. The experience of foreign life thus comes to many an American in the years when he is most impressionable to its stimulus and charm. Berlin and Leipsic, it is true, send back young doctors who are delightfully unconscious how much they must unlearn, but most of them get their bearings again long before they secure their coveted chairs. The years of preliminary training as tutor or assistant are likely to be happy years, too, in spite of drudgery and jealousies and hope deferred. There is the excitement of meeting one's first classes; the first curious glimpse, it may be, into faculty meetings; the first letter addressed to you as " Professor " — you bless the kindly error; the notice of your first paper; the companionship of other young fellows like yourself, already infinitely removed from undergraduate sympathies, and not yet admitted to the inner circle of professorial intimacies. Lucky years, when spurs are to be had for the winning, and when many a teacher, without ever suspecting it, does the best work of his life!

At last, on the red-lettered day of all, comes the professorship, the solid-built chair that is warranted to last, instead of the temporary affair which you now turn over to the next man behind you. You are secure. Barring incapacitating illness, and flagrant violation of the Decalogue, it is a life-appointment. The salary is small, but what there is of it is tolerably certain to be paid; one can marry on it if he has the courage to live plainly. Your lifelong associates will be gentlemen. Your chosen field of work, in science or philosophy or literature, stretches before you in tempting vistas. One-third of the year will be vacation time and hence all your own, — for labor, if your ambition holds, for rest, if you find it flagging. You have the opportunity to impress the best there is in yourself upon a perpetually renewed stream of youthful and more or less ardent minds, and in this thought what satisfaction for the didactic instinct, for the ineradicable schoolmaster that is lurking in us all! Can any profession offer a program half so certain, under normal conditions, of a fair fulfillment? Surely the candle burns brightly at the beginning of the game.

As the years go by, does the college professor regret his choice? I know a few who would gladly change their calling, but only a few, and these are mainly men of energetic, practical cast, who now recognize that by entering another profession they might have quadrupled their income. Men of strong literary and scholarly bent are less likely to question the wisdom of their choice, and indeed, of those outside the college circle, it seems to be the " literary fellows " who speak with most envy of the professor's lot. Aside from lazy midsummer guesses at what one might have been — and who does not hazard these at times? — I find college teachers peculiarly contented.

To turn to the material side of things, the assurance of a fixed income is a source of permanent satisfaction, however disproportionate the income to the service that is rendered. To be sure, the salary of a full professor, the country over, is little if at all in excess of $2000. In the larger universities it may rise to $3000 or something more, but the men who receive above $4000 are so few as to scarcely affect the general average. Aside from the bare possibility of a call to a richer institution, the college professor is not likely to be earning more at fifty than at thirty. Unlike most other professions, there is here no gradual increase of income to give tangible evidence of a man's growth in power. Unless one has taken the Northern Farmer's thrifty advice and " gone where money is " when he married, his outlook as he faces old age is not reassuring. Pensions are extremely rare; college trustees are forced in most cases to be as ungrateful as republics. The cost of living has steadily risen in college towns, keeping pace with the general increase of luxury throughout the older communities. Here and there, particularly in the West, there are exceptions, but upon the whole the scale of necessary expenditure, for a man fulfilling the various social duties required by his position, is constantly growing greater. The professor's incidental income from books and lectures is ordinarily insignificant. When he has paid his bills he finds no margin left for champagne and terrapin. If he smokes at all, he invents ingenious reasons for preferring a pipe. He sees the light-hearted tutors sail for Europe every summer, but as for himself, he decides annually that it will be wiser to wait just one year more. Once in a while he will yield to the temptation to pick up a first edition or a good print, but Aldines and Rembrandt proofs are toys he may not dally with. In short, his tastes are cultivated beyond his income, and his sole comfort is in the Pharisaical reflection that this is better, after all, than to have more income than taste. If his meditations upon quaternions or Descartes or the lyric cry are liable to be interrupted by an insulting cook, striking for another dollar that he can ill spare, it is doubtless a device of Providence to keep him in healthy touch with actualities. It were a pity that in the colleges, of all places, high thinking and plain living should be quite divorced, and that the men whose duty it is to train American boys in citizenship as well as in letters should themselves have no need to practice the stern virtues of industry and thrift.

No man's satisfaction or dissatisfaction with his salary, however, affords a complete indication of his attitude toward his work. A more subtle arithmetic makes up the sum of failure or success. After ten, twenty, or thirty years of experience, the college professor may be analyst enough to pass verdict upon the result of his own efforts, but an outsider's estimate may even then be more accurate than his own. Besides, many a man's point of view becomes insensibly but increasingly modified after he has entered upon his vocation, so that it is difficult for him to decide whether his early ambitions have been realized.

There are two professional types, assuredly, that are admirably adjusted to their environment; the born investigator, and the born teacher. Men belonging to the first of these classes find in research itself a sufficient recompense; their happiness is in widening the bounds of knowledge, and undermining stoutly intrenched stupidities, and adding to the effectiveness of human energy. Almost every college has one or more of these men. The larger institutions have many of them, and the college community is their rightful place. They deserve their bed and board, — and their cakes and ale besides — even if they are too absent-minded to remember their lecture hours, or too feebly magnetic to hold the attention of undergraduates. An unerring process of differentiation is constantly at work, marking out these born scholars and scientists from those of their colleagues who possess scholarly and scientific tastes, but who learn by the time they are forty that they are never likely to produce anything. These latter men often make noteworthy drill-masters. Their respect for original scholarship grows as they come to recognize that it is beyond their own reach. Though they discover the futility of " doing something for " science or literature themselves, they touch elbows daily with men who can, and they reflect something of the glory of it, and impart to their pupils a regard for sound learning.

Not every teacher, of course, is an investigator

THE LIFE OF A COLLEGE PROFESSOR 77

manqué. Your born teacher is as rare as a poet, and as likely to die young. Once in a while a college gets hold of one. It does not always know that it has him, and proceeds to ruin him by over-driving, the moment he shows power; or to let another college lure him away for a few hundred dollars more a year. But while he lasts — and sometimes, fortunately, he lasts till the end of a long life — he transforms the lecture-hall as by enchantment. Lucky is the alumnus who can call the roll of his old instructors, and among the martinets and the pedants and the piously inane can here and there come suddenly upon a man; a man who taught him to think or helped him to feel, and thrilled him with a new horizon.

Sometimes it happens that the great teacher is also a great investigator, but that is a miracle. For a man to be either one or the other — not to speak of being both — requires singular vitality. Outsiders usually underestimate the obstacles to successful professorial work. With regard to one's own scholarly ambitions, particularly, the steady term-time strain, the thankless and idle sessions of committees, the variety of demands upon one's time and energy, combine to make one pay a heavy price for winning distinction. You must do, upon the average, as much teaching as your colleagues, and the time for your *magnum opus* must either be stolen from that due your classes, or you must accomplish two days' work in one. It is true that the number of hours of classroom instruction required of the professor varies greatly in different institutions. Sometimes a schedule of four hours per week is considered sufficient, in the case of men who have won the right to devote themselves to advanced research. In the smaller colleges, and for the younger men in the larger ones, the schedule is often sixteen or twenty hours. Perhaps twelve would be a fair average for colleges and universities the country over. To teach college boys for two hours a day does not seem like a very severe task to one who has never tried it, but I have observed that most professors who have taught or lectured for two hours thoroughly well, putting their best powers into the task, are ready to quit. Few men can rivet the attention of fifty or a hundred students for one hour without feeling, five minutes after the end of it, that vitality has gone out of them. The emery wheel that wears out

THE LIFE OF A COLLEGE PROFESSOR 79

fastest cuts the diamond best; and when a man boasts that he teaches without effort and weariness, he has sufficiently described his teaching. Every college town has its own pitiful or tragic stories of professors who have broken down; they are usually the men whom the college could least afford to lose. It is no wonder that in the face of all this many professors cease trying to ride two horses at once; they either do their duty by their classes and let the dust gather on the leaves of the *magnum opus*, or else they get over their class work with as little expenditure of energy as possible, and give to the *magnum opus* their real strength. And the college would not be the microcosm it is if there were not some professors who abandon both ambitions after a little, becoming quite incurable though often very charming dead-beats; and this, I confess, is the most interesting type of all.

It is a pity that Mark Pattison, whose *Memoirs* throw so terribly frank a light upon the intellectual side of university life, did not leave behind him that essay upon Academic Sterility which I have already suggested that someone ought to write. He may have thought that

Amiel's Journal pictured the malady, for once and all; and certainly Mrs. Humphry Ward, whose Langham is an attempted personification of the class, has succeeded only in clothing with an English garb the self-distrust and impotence of will of the lonely Genevese professor. There can be no reasonable doubt that the academic atmosphere is unfavorable to creative vigor. Few vital books come out of the universities. One cause, beyond question, is the prevalence of the critical spirit.

"Our knowledge petrifies our rhymes."

A sophisticated sense that everything has been written, and better than it is likely to be written again, is not the stuff from which literature is bred. It may be that a mere over-accumulation of material prevents the scholar from ever turning his treasures to account; the monumental treatise becomes arrested, like Mr. Casaubon's, in the pigeon-hole stage. Often, too, he outlives his former intellectual interests, and his drawers are crammed with various half-completed pieces of work, melancholy reminders of enthusiasms that have now grown cold and long years that have been wasted. In morbid self-depreciation or well-grounded despair of making any contribution to the world's thought, and disgusted with class-room routine, many a gifted man, unwilling or unable to resign his chair, turns tramp. Careless of public opinion, he adopts some pet avocation for his vocation henceforth, makes an opiate out of a hobby, and settles down for the rest of his days into a fly-fisherman, or amateur photographer, or cross-country saunterer, or novel reader. But it is then that he is worth knowing! "May God forgive me," cried Sir Walter Scott to his *Diary*, "for thinking that anything can be made out of a schoolmaster!" Ah, shade of Sir Walter, out of a schoolmaster who has survived his illusions and is cheerfully planting his cabbages, there may be made the most delightful companion in the world!

It is because a college faculty exhibits this surprising range of types, illustrative, in little, of almost every variety of success and failure known to the greater world, that it furnishes so perpetually interesting a spectacle. No man who has returned to his own Alma Mater to teach is likely to forget the impressions received at those first faculty meetings, where he has met on terms of absolute equality the gentlemen whose corporate action decided so many vital issues — as it then seemed — in his own undergraduate life. What a revelation to find that "the faculty" are very much like other men: with prejudices and favorite animosities; capable of being much confused by a motion to amend an amendment, and much relieved by a proposition to refer to a committee; the younger ones rigid and the older ones lenient in enforcing the letter of the law; all of them glad to adjourn, and retire to their own toil or their own decorous beer and skittles! But what mastery of parliamentary fence, on the part of old gentlemen who have been making and withdrawing motions for half a century![1] What deep wrath among the disciplinarians over that vote to restore the erring half-back (needed in November) to full standing in his class! What subtle argumentation, pro and con, over Smith's petition to be excused from chapel on the ground of his physician's written statement that Smith's eye-

---

[1] I recall one such expert, who, at the first faculty meeting of the college year, offered a prayer that he and his colleagues might be endowed with "holy skill."

lids are liable to inflammation upon sudden exposure to the morning air! What passionate denunciation of the faculty's past injustice in the famous Robinson case, pronounced by some sunny-tempered philosopher who has just persuaded himself that whenever the student body differs with the faculty on a moral question the students are surely in the right! And is it not singular that over that question of Jones's rank, which any man in the room could settle satisfactorily enough in two minutes if left to himself, two or three dozen educated and experienced gentlemen should sit in futile misery for half an hour, only, at the end of it, to follow sheeplike some obstinate motion that takes them through precisely the wrong hole in the wall? Until the psychology of mobs is better comprehended, there will be no understanding the ways of "faculty action." Even when we shall have learned that the normal powers of the two or three dozen men are under some strange paralyzing inhibition, shall we be able to explain why the inhibition should proceed from the most thick-headed man in the room?

To these gentlemen who grow old in the sheltered academic life, a thousand whimsicalities and petty formalities attach themselves, like barnacles to the bottom of a ship long at anchor. No man can teach ten years and escape them. Unbeknown to himself he is already on the way to becoming a " character," and people are smiling at him in their sleeves. If he finds himself at a reception, he buttonholes a colleague and talks shop. The habit of addressing boys, without contradiction, leaves him often impotent in the sharp give-and-take of talk with men, and many a professor who is eloquent in his classroom is helpless on the street, or in the club, or across the dinner-table. Sometimes he perceives this, and makes pathetic efforts to grow worldly. Faculty circles have been known to experience strange obsessions of frivolity, and to plunge desperately into dancing lessons or duplicate whist. Both the remedy and the disease have their comic aspects, and yet I know of no circles where the twilight hour of familiar talk is more delightful, where common instincts and training and old associations touch the ordinary courtesies of life with a more peculiar charm, where mutual pride is so little spoiled by familiarity, and where lifelong friendships, undisturbed by the accidents frequent in the greater world, grow so intimate and touching as the evil days draw nigh.

A professor's attitude toward the undergraduates is a good test of his personality, but a still better one may be found in their attitude toward him. They are shrewd judges of character, intolerant of shams, and demoniacally ingenious in finding the weak places in a man's armor. If he is a shirk or an ignoramus, they know it as soon as he — perhaps sooner. Your college student is a strange compound of reverence and irreverence, conservative and anarchist, man and boy. If you decide to treat him as a youngster he straightway astonishes you by his maturity; if you thereupon make up your mind to consider him henceforth as a man, he will be guilty of prompt and enthusiastic lapses into juvenility. An American college is half public school, half university. Toward professors whom they like, students are finely loyal, though the curious alternations of popularity which fall to some teachers at the hands of successive classes are quite beyond the reach of analysis. If they do not like a professor, and can get the whip hand over him, undergraduates know how to demonstrate that twenty is the age of perfect cruelty. In few college recitation rooms, nowadays, is there anything said about the whip hand, but it is always there, on one side or the other. Every lecture hall witnesses a daily though possibly unconscious struggle of talent, training, and character against the crowd. The lecturer usually wins, because he knows he must, but many a one who has never experienced defeat invariably rises, like Gough, with knees that tremble. Laboratory and seminary methods of instruction alter these conditions, of course, and bring the professor at once into informal and even intimate relation with his pupils. Upon the whole, the contact with college classes is agreeable to a man of friendly temperament. He learns to make allowance for undergraduate conventionalities, and does not expect enthusiasm where enthusiasm would be bad form. On their part, students generously overlook the whims and crotchets of a favorite professor; they even pardon his amazement at the ways of intercollegiate diplomacy, or his radical skepticism as to the intellectual discipline involved in football.

In one sense, indeed, he is supposed to know very little about the men whom he teaches. The *in loco parentis* theory has long been doomed — at least in the larger institutions — and so far as direct observation is concerned, the professor is as ignorant of what is going on in a student's room as if it were in the South seas. But for all that he can make skillful guesses, from a hundred signs, and when the Seniors file upon the Commencement platform for their degrees, that silent circle of professors often know them better than their mothers do. It is pleasant to meet these fellows afterward, either on the old campus, or at some remote railway junction, or at midnight in a foreign city, and pick up for a moment the dropped threads of acquaintance. Sometimes one learns in these accidental ways that his instruction counted for more than was apparent at the time; he makes the discovery that someone has taken pains to remember words that he himself has long forgotten. Herein lies half the zest of teaching. One blazes away into the underbrush, left barrel and right barrel, vaguely enough as it seems, but some of the shots are sure to tell. Young men are after all so susceptible to impression, so responsive to right feeling, that though the fine reserve of youth may not betray it at the moment, they nevertheless bear away from their instructor the best he has to give them. This may be poor enough, but it is something.

When a professor grows tired of moralizing about his colleagues or his pupils, he always has the president to fall back upon. So have the undergraduates, for that matter, and their parents, and the alumni, and the trustees, and the general public, — and the newspaper reporters. The college president who can conduct himself to the satisfaction of this varied body of critics, and enjoy at the same time the approval of his own conscience, is a gifted man. A president must have many qualifications for his office — I have heard a cautious observer say — but his first need is a thick skin. Undoubtedly, by some wise provision of nature, the skin grows thicker with exposure, but there is a curiously prevalent impression that a president's conscience is liable to a corresponding induration. A cynical-minded friend of mine, of large discourse in these matters, avers that such are the temptations peculiar to the office, that of all the college presidents he has known, only two remained Christians. These two — if I may be permitted to say so without discourtesy to the others — are both dead.

Whatever be the foundation for such impious generalizations, no one will deny that an American college president has a task of extraordinary difficulty. Yet his problems have been met, upon the whole, with consummate skill. Every type of president has done something to advance the cause of higher education in America: the sleek "promoter," the sectarian fanatic, the close-mouthed business manager, the far-sighted educator, the blameless clergyman. These types appear and disappear and blend, but meantime the great cause itself goes lumbering steadily forward.

Two generations ago, the place held by the college professor in the community must have vastly tickled his vanity. Those rules in vogue in New England, requiring students to doff their hats when four rods from a professor (two rods only for a tutor, alas!) were emblematic of the universal homage paid him in a college town. I suppose there is no man so great nowadays, even on great occasions, as those old fellows were continuously. Town and college had a solidarity of interest that is now unknown, except in a few instances of fortunate survival. The commanding position of the professor in the community was often a deserved recognition of his services to the local public. Here and there may still be found a man of the old type, an agitator for all good causes, an orator in town meeting, a politician within the bounds of dignity, but it is a common complaint among the townspeople in academic communities that your modern professor is a Gallio. He may turn out occasionally to manifest his interest in some crisis of the church or school or state, but in general he sticks to his library. This criticism is often short-sighted, particularly in reference to politics. The professor who patiently teaches his classes, week in and week out, to think straight, to see that two and two make four on either side of the Atlantic and that " stealing will continue stealing," serves his country better than a hundred " spell-binders " in the last frantic days of a campaign. But upon the whole there is ground for the current complaint as to the college teacher's unconcern for public questions. He remains in one sense a leading figure in his community. There are certain things he may not do without losing caste. The butcher, with a vague feeling of his importance, charges him a couple of extra cents per pound, and the suave Armenian refugee, noting the real Bokhara on his floor, pockets the professorial gift of two dollars and thinks in his Oriental heart that it ought to have been five. Yet in these respects he may be a marked man — unluckily! — without possessing any of the old, real leadership of influence and character. Plausible as may be his excuses of preoccupation with wider intellectual interests, the tone of American civic life has already suffered from his indifference. There are indications, however, of a reaction against this indolent exclusiveness. It may be that the hour of selfish acquisition and ungenerous rivalry between the colleges is passing, and that side by side they are to strive once more, and more effectively than ever, for the common welfare. Some such aspiration is certain to thrill sooner or later, the loneliest scholar in the most secluded corner of the college world; for even the inveterate pedant may possess a "most public soul."

After all is said, the life of a college professor presents, under curious disguises, the old, universal issues. It is a noble profession for the noble-hearted, and but a petty calling for a man of petty mind.

COLLEGE PROFESSORS AND THE PUBLIC

COLLEGE PROFESSORS AND THE PUBLIC

In a recent number of the *Harvard Graduates' Magazine* there is a sketch entitled "A Harvard Ascetic." It describes that singular gentleman and scholar, Evangelinus Apostolides Sophocles, with whose academic career anecdote and myth have long been busy. For some thirty-six years after his appointment as Greek tutor, in 1842, Professor Sophocles "lived by himself," we are told, "in the west entry of Holworthy, and there cooked and spread his frugal meals, amid his lexicons and papers and exercise books." Whether he bred his famous chickens in his sleeping room is still a matter for high debate among Cambridge humorists of an antiquarian turn. At any rate he seems to have lived his own life in serene indifference to contemporary opinion. He preserved throughout the most stirring period of the last century the spiritual isolation of the exile. He remained from first to last a Greek monk, set to the somewhat incongruous task of teaching American boys.

I am so unfortunate as never to have known Evangelinus Apostolides Sophocles. But I have often been inclined to moralize upon his monastic existence, in comparing it with the fuller if more interrupted lives of some of his contemporaries and pupils. For there have been many grammarians quite as anxious as Professor Sophocles to "settle Hoti's business" and impart "the doctrine of the enclitic *de*," who have cheerfully surrendered their scanty hours for research at the call of public service; arguing in town meetings for better schoolhouses and better roads, visiting and burying the town poor, securing better terms from the all-invading trolley companies, addressing legislative committees in behalf of local improvements, — sparing, in short, no time or labor where the expenditure of time and labor might insure better conditions of living for the communities where the scholar's lot was cast. That this devotion to the claims of the town or city or general public is likely to interfere with Hoti's business is undeniable. The doctrine of the enclitic *de* is less clearly defined to-day than it might have been if all college teachers had lived, like Professor Sophocles, in the west entry of a dormitory, engrossed with lexicons and exercise books, and with a few chickens, possibly, to add speculative interest to the scene. There is, one must confess, a more or less constant antinomy between the instincts of pure scholarship and the impulses of citizenship. It is a warfare which accounts, at least in part, for the peculiar status of the college professor under the conditions of contemporary American life; and certain phases of the rather complex situation growing out of these contradictory duties one may venture to discuss.

Few educated men will deny the imaginative charm that invests the existence of the solitary scholar. In his person we discover one man, in this confusing world, who knows what he likes. Chaucer's Clerk of Oxenford, who had

"levere have at his beddes heede
Twenty bookes, clad in blak or reede
Of Aristotle and his philosophie
Than robes riche, or fithele, or gay sawtrie,"

is something more than a type of mediæval devotion to the Aristotelian logic. Some breath of his ascetic spirit still abides in every scholar worthy of the name; the twenty books continue to yield to such a man a deeper delight than the robes or the fiddle. There is no college faculty without its Clerk of Oxenford, — some unworldly soul who grows old without tangible rewards, possibly without very tangible achievements, but who has nevertheless kept the pure flame of learning alive in his heart. Innocent eccentricities attach themselves to him. Young doctors from the great foreign and American universities find him a trifle old-fashioned in his views and unaware of the latest dissertations. Yet the blameless Clerk loves his twenty books to the end.

One such man I remember in particular. In his younger days he had been a Latinist, until the loss, by fire, of his manuscript Latin grammar disheartened him, and he accepted a casual offer of a chair of elementary mathematics, which he kept till his death. He fulfilled his duties as instructor with perfect gravity and fidelity, but cared wholly for other things: for his collections of Phædrus and black-letter Chaucers; for Scott's novels, which he used to read through once each year; for the elder dramatists; for Montaigne and Lamb. Weather permitting, he drove from twenty to forty miles a day in his rusty, mud-covered buggy; he knew every wild flower, every lovely or bold view, within reach of Williamstown. To be his companion upon one of these drives was to touch the very essence of fine, whimsical, irresponsible scholarship. But Professor Dodd made no speeches in town meeting, was scantily interested in no-license agitation, was rather likely to forget election day altogether, and on pleasant Sundays used to patronize obscure churches that lay at an extraordinary driving distance from home. His sense of freedom from these compulsions that are laid upon the strenuous citizen of New England was very charming. The land of his habitation was "far from this our war."

The type of moral detachment which my old friend thus exemplified is not only charming; it is positively necessary, if the work demanded by productive scholarship — though he was quite frankly an unproductive scholar! — is adequately to be done. It is an encumbrance to the scholar, as it is to the soldier, to entangle himself overmuch with the affairs of this life. Certain members of every academic community seem drafted by nature and by achievement to special service. They are summoned out of the usual social order, away from the conventional, wholesome round of ordinary discipline, to lead some forlorn hope of science or letters, to explore the farthest boundaries of human knowledge, to chart unknown waters that will by and by be crowded with the funnels of the carrying trade of the world. There is a profound sense in which every such man must, like Newton, be

"forever
Voyaging through strange seas of thought alone."

He cannot keep in touch with the normal life of other men. If he brings back something to us at the end of his voyages, that is enough; he must not be held to rigid attendance upon ward meetings and Sunday school. The chances are that not twenty men in the world will recognize, at first, what these explorations mean to human progress; their significance is realized very gradually. Meantime the man's neighbors will know merely that he is gone, — that he is absent-minded, forgetful of jury duty and registration and a hundred admirable "causes."

Since this type of intellectual pioneer is so essential to the true progress of the race, there is no likelihood that it will not persist. Indeed, there are more opportunities open to it and greater honors are paid to it to-day, in this country, than we have ever offered before. The Clerk of Oxenford, who was "not right fat," as it may be remembered, in the fourteenth century, is better clothed and fed and housed in the twentieth. Yet the college teachers who really make original contributions to human knowledge are few in proportion to the total numbers engaged in the profession. The passion for scholarship, like that for poetry, does not always imply a corresponding power of production; and because we are glad to release some picked man from the common social obligations and services, and bid him Godspeed upon his adventure, it does not follow that a similar freedom may be claimed for those who stay at home. The solitary scholar will always be the exception, not the rule. The college professor, under normal conditions, can escape neither his duties to the public nor the daily irresistible impact from the public. His endeavor to escape them may be an evidence of instinctive capacity for creative work of the highest value; but it has not infrequently been the badge of a mere Bohemianism, a mark of the reckless, selfish existence of an alien, — of a man with no stake in the community.

"I do not often speak to public questions," said Emerson, who, without formal academic relations, was nevertheless in so many ways our finest type of academic behavior: "they are odious and hurtful, and it seems like meddling or leaving your work. I have my own spirits in prison, — spirits in deeper prisons, whom no man visits if I do not. And then I see what havoc it makes with any good mind, a dissipated philanthropy. The one thing not to be forgiven to intellectual persons is, not to know their own task."

Yet these serene sentences were uttered at the opening of his address on the Fugitive Slave Law, and he goes on to say that he never felt the crack of the slaveowner's whip until that measure, backed as it was by Daniel Webster, put a check on his free speech and action. Then, with words fairly incandescent with noble scorn, Emerson denounces a law which he believes to be an outrage alike upon the rights of private citizenship and upon the public honor. That speech upon the Fugitive Slave Law deserves to be read with the more famous Phi Beta Kappa oration of 1837 on the American Scholar. The earlier address describes the scholar's duty toward his work; the speech of 1854 states and exemplifies the scholar's duty as a citizen.

Scarcely half a century has elapsed since these later words of Emerson were spoken. Yet what far-reaching changes have been wrought in the relations of the academic scholar to the public! Many of the most characteristic phases of our modern industrial and social development are less than half a century old. Within that period the curriculum of the American college has been transformed. The professor of to-day, instead of occupying himself solely with the dead languages and a little mathematics and philosophy, pursues studies and gives instruction that bring him into touch, at a thousand points of contact, with the material interests, the practical concerns, of the American public. Some Evangelinus Apostolides Sophocles still trims his solitary lamp in every college; and in every college there are still, as always, men whose instincts of citizenship are wholly independent of the work of their particular department. But a newer type of college professor is also everywhere in evidence: the expert who knows all about railroads and bridges and subways; about gas commissions and electrical supplies; about currency and banking, Philippine tariffs, Venezuelan boundary lines, the industries of Porto Rico, the classification of the civil service, the control of trusts. I take my illustrations almost at random, and yet in connection with each topic upon that variegated list it would be possible to point to college professors who have lately been rendering a signal public service. These men combine technical training with practical capacity. They can no longer be brushed aside contemptuously as "mere theorists." They are helping to carry forward the detailed work of governmental departments; and as you and I are paying for their traveling expenses and their stenographers, they ought to meet every American definition of "the practical man"!

And we must take into account other facts besides these new professorial activities springing out of the new scientific and commercial energy

COLLEGE PROFESSORS AND THE PUBLIC 105

of the nation. This energy has been felt by the universities, and it has produced university men who, judged by any previous academic standards, belong to a new species. But the college professor who represents the " humanities " rather than the distinctly scientific side of modern education, is likewise brought closer to the public than ever before. The newspapers report — and misreport — him. Editors offer him space to reply. Publishers weary him with appeals to write text-books. He goes to conventions. He has become sophisticated. The great festivals of his university — like the rural college Commencements of sixty years ago — assume the character of a popular show. The President of the United States attends them. The professor's photograph, in full academic costume, assaults your eye in the market-place. The college press club and the university's bureau of publicity give his lecture dates in advance. The prospectus of your favorite magazine bids you inspect his literary qualifications as well as his thoughtful countenance. *Who's Who in America* informs you of the name of his second wife.

In all this familiarity of intercourse with the

world, some of the fine old reserve of manner and reticence of speech has been lost. The secularized professor — like one of those gray Italian convents now secularized into orphan schools — is sometimes rather a noisy, middle-class affair. Yet if something of the traditional fastidiousness and exclusiveness has disappeared, other qualities, more robust, and probably more useful, have been gained. It has been an advantage to the public to see the professor at closer range, and it has been a still more obvious benefit to the professor himself that he has found manifold modes of contact with his fellow citizens. For the lessons which the professor learns from the public are at least as important as those which he imparts. If, as the cant phrase has it, he does something occasionally to "purify politics," politics pretty constantly clarifies him.

This growth in mutual knowledge between a single class in the community and the community as a whole has already proved its value, but the limits of its usefulness have by no means been reached. Popular suspicion of the political theorist — a suspicion curiously active at the present moment — is still apt to find in the " college professor" a convenient symbol of ineptitude. The Philistinism which glorifies the so-called " man of action " minimizes by contrast the man of thought. Nor is it to be expected that the general public can ever develop a full sympathy with the academic scholar whose mind is bent solely upon discovering the truth. It may respect him if he keeps out of the way. But let him once lift his voice against some popular movement, and the hisses will be prompt enough. Most of us can remember the time when college professors of economics who advocated tariff for revenue were stigmatized as " British emissaries " with their pockets stuffed with " British gold." There is less said just now about British emissaries, and yet the college economist who does not, in football parlance, " buy the winning colors after the game" must still pay the penalty of his hardihood. College teachers have been openly denounced as " traitors " for advocating self-government for the Filipinos. In many a pulpit and newspaper office, it was declared that the utterances of college professors were largely responsible for the assassination of President McKinley. Singularly enough, the most bitter denunciations of the college professor in politics come from college-trained politicians and journalists; there is no such master of the sneer as the partisan who in his youth

> " did eagerly frequent
> Doctor and saint."

In short, courage is still necessary if the college teacher desires to speak frankly upon disputable topics. In 1904 it is easy to be a champion of the gold standard, because the gold standard has fortunately prevailed; in 1896 the comfort of such a championship depended upon the longitude of the college. We are gradually learning to analyze the complex elements that enter into the question of " academic freedom," and to discover that human nature must not be left out of the reckoning; but meantime it must be confessed that academic freedom, like the Supreme Court in Mr. Dooley's epigram, " follows the election returns."

Yet there is something to be said for that instinct of self-preservation which forces the majority, in a democracy like ours, to silence demonstrative opposition, and proceed with the public affairs. One must admit that a good many college professors have taken the Irish members of Parliament as their exemplars, and are boyishly pleased if they can merely obstruct the business of the House. Miss Fanny Burney once wrote of Sir Philip Jennings Clerk, "He is a professed minority man." This type of man is familiar in academic circles. There is something very admirable in his bravery, in his consistency, and in the Cato-like — the Oxford-like — pride with which he clings to lost causes. But, like all of us, he needs to discriminate. John Milton, who was "a professed minority man" of the most militant order, declared that "when God commands to take the trumpet, and blow a dolorous or a jarring blast, it lies not in man's will what he shall say or what he shall conceal." Noble, heartening words are these, and as much needed now as ever. Yet there should be a reasonable certainty that the note is really blown at God's command; and one may concede that the professed minority man of the academic species sometimes mistakes for the Divine clarion what is merely a tin trumpet hanging on the wall of his private study, and that he blows it mainly for the exercise of his lungs.

It is easy to comprehend, and it should be easy to pardon, these professorial extravagances. They are the excitable utterances of men not habitually sobered by practical contact with affairs. Yet an excited participation in public debate is better, after all, than indifference ; and as the solidarity of interests between all classes in the republic becomes more generally realized, there is likely to be less and less criticism of academic critics. While making fullest admission of the occasional peevishness and exaggeration of these men, it should never be forgotten that no class of American citizens bring to the discussion of current questions so wide a knowledge of the teachings of history, a deeper attachment to American ideals, and a more disinterested patriotism.

The field of political activity has been selected to illustrate some of the relations of the professor with the public, not only because the illustration lies conveniently near at hand, but also because it is typical of other activities as well. The benefits that have attended the more general participation of college teachers in current politics are undeniable. They justify the belief that many of the obstructions which still embarrass the commerce of the professor with the public will disappear upon better mutual acquaintance. There are many spheres of public activity in which college teachers need encounter none of the suspicion that is bred by partisan politics. In the fight for better tenements, for public parks, bath-houses, libraries, and training-schools; in all the varied work of philanthropic, ethical, and religious organizations; in the immense task of securing and developing throughout this country a respect for law, a man is not handicapped because he earns his living in a college. He will discover, if he makes the effort, that he can come to closer quarters with his fellow Americans, not only without abandoning any old ideals worth keeping, but with the certainty of obtaining an invigorating supply of new ideals. His working hours may be devoted to investigation or to classroom instruction; he may hope to influence his generation through his pupils or through his books; but he will have at least certain moments of leisure. These may be spent, if he will, in widening his knowledge of the American people of to-day.

I have already referred to one delightful Williamstown personage, the late Professor Dodd, as an instance of academic detachment. I shall choose a phrase descriptive of a more normal scheme of life from a remark made about another resident of the Berkshire college town, named "Russ" Pratt. He was the one-armed and more stupid brother of the half-witted and locally famous "Bill" Pratt. As Russ was reputed to be the laziest man in Williamstown, — a village that had many claimants to that distinction, — I once asked his adopted daughter how her father spent his time. Her answer was epigrammatic in its swiftness and scope: "He saws wood, sets in the house, and goes down street!" Is not that an admirable formula? Labor, reflection, social contact! Could there be a wiser counsel of perfection for the college professor? Poor fellow, he must "saw wood" or freeze; yet he has some opportunity to reflect, in a world which is just now little enough given to reflection; and surely he might "go down street" more often and to better advantage than he does. The street no less than the library has its whims, partialities, extravagances, panics. But the man of the library has much to learn from the man of the street, and a riper friendship between them will betoken a better service toward their common country.

A friend of James Russell Lowell has said that in Lowell's later life he sometimes spoke discontentedly of the years he had spent as a college professor. He complained humorously that he had been wont, in those earlier days, to lecture for an hour or two, go back to Elmwood, fill his pipe, and thank God that he had done a day's work. Now it is not easy to say what shall constitute a day's work, either for one's self or for another; the question is not so simple as the arithmetic of the labor unions would seem to imply. Yet that is a scant day's work, whether long or short, that does not bring the worker into some relation to human progress; that does not make men and women freer, wiser, better. Lowell's years of service in the Smith Professorship may have been as fruitful as any years of his life, although it was the nobler side of him, no doubt, that made him question it.

But who knows the pattern into which his days and years are being woven? I remember complaining, long ago, to a venerable professor, as we were walking together to morning chapel, that a required chapel service involved a costly expenditure of time; and that the German scholars were steadily drawing ahead of their American rivals because, for one reason, they saved that half hour a day. His reply was very fine: "If you are turning a grindstone, every moment is precious; but if you are doing a man's work, the inspired moments are precious." Every fully endowed man believes that saying in his heart, whatever he may think about the specific question of compulsory chapel for the college-bred; and as our modern world gradually reveals to us both its complexity and its spiritual unity, the "inspired moments" are increasingly likely to be those, not of lonely intuition, but of organized social service. No Americans, above all, no body of educated Americans, should imagine that they have a charter to live unto themselves. The whole contemporary movement is against it, — the secularization of knowledge, the democratization of society, the fundamental oneness of interest among all peoples of this swiftly narrowing earth. For the members of any profession to insulate themselves from these currents of world-sympathy is to cut off that profession's power. The astonishing development of academic studies in our day, the evolution of these new types of professorial activity, the immense endowments and other evidences of public interest in the American college, are fortunate auguries for the republic. But they are also welcome because they invite the professor himself to make generous contribution to what the President of Harvard, in speaking at the bicentennial of Yale, characterized as "the pervasive, aggressive, all-modifying spirit of Christian democracy."

HAWTHORNE AT NORTH ADAMS

HAWTHORNE AT NORTH ADAMS

THE westward-bound passenger on the Fitchburg Railroad, emerging from the long roar of the Hoosac Tunnel, sees the smoke-blurred electric lamps quenched in sudden daylight, shuts his watch, and finds himself in North Adams. The commercial travelers leave the car, and a boy comes in with the Troy papers. A grimy station hides the close-built town, though upon the left one can see row above row of boarding-houses clinging to the face of a rocky foothill of Greylock, and further to the south a bit of meadow land not yet covered with railroad sidings. Then the train moves on, and in a moment plunges into another tunnel, and so out of the Tunnel City.

Thirty years ago, the traveler's first glimpse of North Adams was more picturesque. The big six-horse coaches, starting from Rice's, away over in the winding valley of the Deerfield, and climbing Hoosac Mountain, used to swing at full gallop along the two or three miles of tableland on the summit of the range, past the queer old houses of Florida, the highest township in Massachusetts, and pull up for a moment where the road turned sharply down the western slope. On the right were the last reluctant spurs of the Green Mountains; directly in front, over the broad Williamstown valley, stretched the clear-cut Taconics; at the left rose the massive lines of Greylock. At one's feet, far below, were two or three church spires, and the smoke of factories. Tiny houses were already perching here and there on the steep sides of the mill streams; for North Adams has no site whatever, and from the beginning has had to climb for its life. Completely enfolded by hills as the village seemed, one could yet catch a glimpse, as the driver gathered up his reins for the long descent, of a valley extending southward, between Ragged Mountain and the Hoosac range, toward the towns of lower Berkshire.

It was up this valley, more than half a century ago, that the Pittsfield stage brought Hawthorne to North Adams. He was taking, in rather aimless fashion, one of those summer outings, which gave him more pleasure, he said, than other people had in the whole year beside. Nothing drew him to northern Berkshire, apparently, except the mere chance of travel; but he found the place congenial, and there are facts connected with his stay there that throw a clear light upon Hawthorne, at a period critical both for himself and his art. There are persons still living who well remember his sojourn in North Adams. His favorite companions were men prominent in the little community, and of such marked personal qualities that story and legend are busy with them to this hour; so that even if the graphic delineations of the *American Note-Books* were not at hand, one might still form a fairly accurate picture of the North Adams of 1838.

Halfway down the straggling main street, upon the site of the present Wilson House, was a noted inn, called either after its proprietor, Smith's Tavern, or according to its politics, the Whig Tavern, or else, and more pretentiously, the North Adams House. Those were the days of Martin Van Buren, and the Democratic, or Waterman Tavern, was across the way, on the corner now occupied by the Richmond House. But Hawthorne, though on the very eve of becoming a Democratic office-holder, weakly yielded to the attractions of the Whig Tavern, being doubtless lured by the reputation of Orrin Smith as a hotel-keeper. Up to the many-pillared piazza of Smith's Tavern drove the stages from Greenfield and Pittsfield, from Troy and Albany. The broad stoop was the favorite loafing-place of the village characters. Here sat mild-mannered Captain Carter, with butternut meats and maple sugar for sale in little tin measures, which Hawthorne has described with curious precision; and which descended, by the way, after the captain's death, to a well-known vagrant in the adjoining village of Williamstown. Hither hobbled " Uncle John " Sheldon, the Revolutionary pensioner. Here was to be found the one-armed soap-maker, Daniel Haynes, nicknamed " Black Hawk," who had once been a lawyer, and had been ruined by drink, though there was still " a trace of the gentleman and man of intellect " in him. And here, accompanied by his Newfoundland dog, was the brandy-possessed " Doctor Bob " Robinson, a sort of fearless and savage Falstaff, the fame of whose single combats and evil ways and miraculous gifts of healing lingers even yet in the Tunnel City.

Along the piazza, or within the hospitable barroom, sat village worthies of a higher grade: Otis Hodge the millwright, Orrin Witherell the blacksmith, Squire Putnam and Squire Drury and the rest, filling their broad-bottomed chairs with the dignity acquired by years of habitude. Jovial old fellows were these patrons of the Whig Tavern, — Rhode Island Baptists, most of them, — hard-handed and level-headed, with hearty laughs and strongly flavored stories, with coarse appetites for meat and drink, and "a tendency to obesity." Doubtless they scrutinized each new arrival, drew shrewd inferences as to his occupation and character, and decided whether he was worthy of their intimacy. We do not know their first impressions of the young man who stepped out of the Pittsfield stage on the 26th of July, but there is every evidence that he was strongly attracted to these broad-backed tavern-haunters, and was promptly initiated into their circle. Curiously enough, their new friend was the most delicately imaginative genius this country has yet produced; gifted with such elusive qualities, such swift, bright, fairy-like fancies, that his college mates had nicknamed him "Oberon;" so shy and solitary that for years he had scarcely gone upon the streets of his native town except at night; so modest that he concealed his identity as a story-writer under a dozen different signatures; with a personal reserve so absolute and insistent that no liberty was ever taken with him; beautiful in face and form, fresh-hearted and pure-souled. A strange associate, indeed, for Orrin Witherell and Otis Hodge, Orrin Smith and "Doctor Bob" Robinson! Ragged, one-armed "Black Hawk," soap-boiler and phrenologist, stopped in his "wild and ruined and desperate talk" to look at the new guest. "My study is man," he said. "I do not know your name, but there is something of the hawk-eye about you, too." And thus the two students of man entered into fellowship.

Hawthorne tarried at the North Adams House until the 11th of September. He bathed in the pools along Hudson's Brook, and climbed the hills at sunset. He chatted on the tavern stoop with "Uncle John" Sheldon and with Captain Carter, of whose name he was not quite certain, and which he enters in the journal as "I believe, Capt. Gavett." On rainy days he sat in the barroom and consorted with Methodistical cattle drovers, stage agents, agents for religious and abolition newspapers, and an extraordinary variety of other people. He attended court, the menagerie, and the funeral of a child. Sometimes he took brief excursions in the neighborhood; as, for instance, to the Williams Commencement. Here he might have seen Mark Hopkins, presiding for the second time, flanked by dignitaries of the church and state; he might have listened to twenty-three orations, upon themes of which *The Influence of Deductive and Inductive Habits on the Character*, by William Bross, and *The Effect of Music on the Feelings*, by Henry M. Field, are perhaps fair examples, — to say nothing of the polished periods of the Rev. Orville Dewey's address before the alumni. But, as a matter of fact, this conscienceless graduate of Bowdoin apparently spent most of his time behind the church, watching the peddlers and the negroes. The only evidence that he entered the big white meeting-house at all is his remark that there were well-dressed ladies there, "the sunburnt necks in contiguity with the delicate fabrics of the dresses showing the yeoman's daughters."

Some of the people with whom the usually taciturn Hawthorne conversed, in the course of his walks and drives, made a deep impression upon his imagination. Of an old man whose children were connected with a circus establishment, he noted, as Wordsworth might have done, " While this old man is wandering among the hills, his children are the gaze of multitudes." On the top of Hoosac Mountain he met, one day, a German Jew, traveling with a diorama. After Hawthorne had looked at it, a curious elderly dog made his appearance, which the romance-writer has described with such extreme fidelity as to give Mr. Henry James the impression of a " general vacancy in the field of Hawthorne's vision," although it will appear that Hawthorne knew what he was about. One moonlight night he ascended the mountain side, startling the lonely watcher by one of those huge lime-kilns that then, and for many years, abounded near North Adams; and, going up to the top of the kiln, the future author of *Ethan Brand* gazed

HAWTHORNE AT NORTH ADAMS

down upon the red-hot marble, burning with its "bluish, lambent flame." Experiences like this were destined to reappear, more or less transformed, in his creative work; but often the incidents recorded in the journal are of the very simplest character, as, for instance, the fact that two little girls, bearing tin pails, who met him on the Notch road, "whispered one another and smiled."

North Adams is a strange place, after all, to find Oberon in, — Oberon, the king of the fairies. We are not likely to understand the secret of Hawthorne's stay there unless we remember that the summer of 1838 was the most important epoch of his life.

What is first to be observed in the North Adams portion of the *American Note-Books* is the professional point of view. The writer is an artist in search of material. "Conceive something tragical to be talked about," he adds, after describing the old man whose children were in the circus, "and much might be made of this interview in a wild road among the hills." He notes elsewhere: "A little boy named Joe, who haunts about the bar-room and the stoop, four years old, in a thin, short jacket, and full-breeched trousers, and bare feet. . . . Take this boy as the germ of a tavern-haunter, a country *roué*, to spend a wild and brutal youth, ten years of his prime in the state prison, and his old age in the poorhouse." Thus generously does the Hawthorne who himself haunts the Whig Tavern suggest to that other Hawthorne who invents stories that he might "take this boy." The suggestion was adopted, though Joe was not made to run through the melancholy course so vividly outlined for him; and readers of the *Note-Books*, who have wondered what ever became of the little fellow, — whose real name was not Joe, but Edward, — will doubtless be glad to learn that he grew up to be an eminently respectable citizen, and moved West! But the paragraph about Joe is a typical one.

Hawthorne was thirty-four years old that summer, and for a dozen years had devoted himself, in a solitary and more or less ineffective way, to the art of fiction. A gentleman who well remembers his sojourn at the North Adams House says that he used to walk along the street with his eyes down, and that he presented the tavern-keeper's niece with a book he had written. This book, published the year before, was *Twice-Told Tales*. In Hawthorne's well-known criticism upon these stories, written many years afterward, he accounted for their negative character — "the pale tint of flowers that blossomed in too retired a shade" — by his way of life while composing them. It had been a hermit life, a life of shadows, yet now and then of almost pathetic grasping after realities. The articles in *Twice-Told Tales* which pleased the author best were those elaborate exercises in description, valuable indeed as illustration of the accuracy of Hawthorne's self-training in detailed observation, but more valuable as evidences of his struggle to turn from his air-drawn fancies, and morbid though often extremely powerful imaginings, to the common sunshine, the trivial sweet realities of the actual world.

Now, the author of the North Adams journal is the Hawthorne of the *Toll-Gatherer's Day* and *Little Annie's Ramble*, rather than the Hawthorne of the *Prophetic Pictures* and *Fancy's Show Box*. He turns eagerly to the life about him; he notes its details with fascinated interest. Nothing comes amiss to him; the long valley of the Notch, as it sweeps up to the Bellowspipe, and a grunting drove of pigs passing the tavern at dusk, are alike entered in his note-book. Fifty years before the preface to *Pierre et Jean* was written, here was a young man in an obscure corner of Massachusetts practicing a " theory of observation " which would have satisfied De Maupassant himself. The extraordinary precision of Hawthorne's descriptions thus early in his career can be fully appreciated only by one who discovers how a mere line from the *Note-Books* will to-day serve, with the older citizens of North Adams, to identify the village characters sketched therein; or by one who will stand, with Hawthorne's words before him, by the side of Hudson's Brook, or on the desolate summit of Bald Mountain, or at that point on the Notch road where there is a view of Williamstown, " with high, mountainous swells heaving themselves up, like immense subsiding waves, far and wide around it."

There was a reason for this passion for the outer world. Solitude had done its utmost for Hawthorne, at least for the time being, and he had come to a parting of the ways. A single sentence from a letter to an intimate friend in

1838 is like a cry from the man's inmost soul, — "I want to have something to do with the material world." Wedged in between Otis Hodge and Orrin Witherell around the huge fire in the public room of the Whig Tavern, his elbows touching those stout-built, cheery-souled embodiments of pioneer virtues and vices, and casting himself into the life of the village in all its varied activities, Hawthorne found the "material world" with which he longed to come in touch. When he left North Adams, it was to enter almost at once upon the life of a weigher and gauger in the Boston Custom House, and to stand thenceforth in the ranks with his fellow-men.

But Hawthorne's new contact with actualities was something more than a mere quickening of interests, a broadening of his range, a closer focusing of his professional eye upon the object. He was a writer; he had the passion for observing, recording, recombining; he could not help it. It may well be that when such a man throws himself upon the actual, the result is simply a keener physical vision, a more perfect analysis, a more pitiless art. This fate was quite possible for Hawthorne. The fear of it haunted him, and never more so than in this very year when he made his escape from it. He wrote to Longfellow, "There is no fate in this world so horrible as to have no share in its joys and sorrows." To the mere observer as well as to the mere dreamer — and Hawthorne had been both by turns — may come that paralysis which lays hold of the very roots of life and art together; which begins in artistic detachment, and ends in the sterility of isolation. From the horror of that death in life, which has fallen in our day upon artists like Flaubert and his more brilliant nephew, Hawthorne was saved, as he believed, by the influence of the woman who afterward became his wife. In his own simple phrase, his heart was touched. "I used to think I could imagine all passions, all feelings and states of the heart and mind, but how little did I know! Indeed, we are but shadows; we are not endowed with real life; and all that seems most real about us is but the thinnest substance of a dream till the heart be touched. That touch creates us; then we begin to be; thereby we are beings of reality and inheritors of eternity."

Hawthorne had already felt that creative touch

in the summer of 1838. It accounts — does it not ? — for the new sense of reality so apparent in the journal. It was not simply his artistic interest, but his sympathy, that started into a quicker life. His extraordinarily sensitive mind brooded upon the risk he had run of becoming a cool observer, untaught that he had a heart; it became, in his own words, "a fearful thought" to him, and, being an artist to the finger-tips, he put his fearful thought into artistic form. In *Ethan Brand*, the story of the man who committed the Unpardonable Sin, Hawthorne embodied not only his North Adams character studies, but the very emotion that must have stirred his deepest heart during those weeks of sojourn at the Whig Tavern. He laid upon the shoulders of the lime-burner on the slope of Hoosac the awful burden whose weight he himself had almost felt.

Ethan Brand, a Chapter from an Abortive Romance, was first published in the *Dollar Magazine* under the title of *The Unpardonable Sin*, in 1851. The date of its composition is uncertain. Mr. Lathrop thinks that Hawthorne's removal to Berkshire in 1850 may have revived his interest in the old material provided by the *Note-Books ;*

Mr. Conway is inclined to believe that the story was written in 1848. Nor is it clear how literally the subtitle is to be taken. There are allusions in *Ethan Brand* to preceding episodes connected with the theme, of such dramatic possibilities that Hawthorne may well have sketched them in his fancy, but whether he ever seriously tried his hand upon anything more than the culminating chapter is doubtful. Two things, however, are certain: for the setting of the story, its author drew exclusively upon notes taken in North Adams; and the moral problem involved in it was Hawthorne's own problem, as a man and an artist, in the summer of 1838. Remembering how long he brooded over the *Septimius Felton* theme and the *Scarlet Letter* theme before writing a word, it will not seem improbable that the conception of *Ethan Brand* should date from the time of his first visit to Berkshire, even if the story remained unwritten for a dozen years; though, as a matter of fact, it is not at all unlikely that its composition is to be placed much earlier than the critics have surmised.

Ostensibly a fragment, and undoubtedly bearing internal evidence of some haste or dissatisfaction on the author's part, *Ethan Brand* remains one of the most powerful things that Hawthorne ever wrote. Rarely has he shown such dramatic instinct as when he marshaled his old North Adams acquaintances into the moonshine and narrow streaks of firelight that illuminated the open space before the lime-kiln on the sombre mountain side. They are all there: the stage agent, the crippled soap-boiler, the brandy-possessed doctor, the old man whose daughter had wandered away with the circus, the German Jew with his diorama, and the curious old dog. It is little Joe who guides them into the presence of their former associate, Ethan Brand, who has committed " the one only crime for which Heaven can afford no mercy." Many notes from the journal are adopted without change. Sometimes there is a mere shifting of descriptive phrases that seem to suit Hawthorne's fancy; as when the " wild and ruined and desperate talk " attributed in the *Note-Books* to the cripple is here given to the doctor; or the sentence " Earth was so mingled with sky that it was a day-dream to look at it," originally written of Williamstown, is applied to the village of the tale. But there are more subtle adaptations of his material in two allusions to events not narrated in the story itself, however definitely Hawthorne may have outlined them in his imagination. The old man's missing daughter has become " the Esther of our tale," " whom with such cold and remorseless purpose Ethan Brand had made the subject of a psychological experiment." Reference is also made to "a professional visit of the village doctor to Ethan Brand, during the latter's supposed insanity." Hawthorne has perhaps wrought out the psychological experiment motive often enough elsewhere to indicate what would probably have been his method here; but the idea of bringing " Doctor Bob," with his huge animalism and mordant humor, " savage as a wild beast and miserable as a lost soul," to minister to the spiritual malady that preyed upon Ethan Brand, might easily have resulted in a scene unmatched in the whole range of Hawthorne's work.

If it is a pure bit of romanticism to transform the Jew of Hoosac Mountain to " the Jew of Nuremberg," the mask of the fiend himself, there is, on the other hand, in the description of the antics of the old dog an instance of the power of

Hawthorne's realism. In the *Note-Books*, the trivial incident of the dog's chasing his own tail is minutely narrated, as a fact somehow worth recording. In *Ethan Brand*, the fact is nothing except as it illustrates a truth: the man who had chased the world over for something that was in his own breast, " moved by a perception of some remote analogy between his own case and that of the self-pursuing cur," broke into the awful laugh that sent the jovial party hurrying homewards through the darkening woods.

For Ethan Brand himself there is no model in the journal. None was needed. Hawthorne's own problem, in that critical year, was to keep " the counterpoise between his mind and heart." The doom he dreaded most of all was, to be " no longer a brother man, opening the chambers or the dungeons of our common nature by the key of holy sympathy, which gave him a right to share in all its secrets," but to be, like Ethan Brand, " a cold observer, looking on mankind as the subject of his experiment." The scene of the tale is the very hillside where Hawthorne wandered, brooding over the isolation that kills and the touch that makes alive. Its personages are the people that jostled against him in the tavern. But Hawthorne found Ethan Brand — or a potential Ethan Brand — in his own heart. He believed in an Unpardonable Sin; and it is by this faith in the reality of the moral life, after all is said, that he takes his rank as an artist. He chose moral problems, the truths of the human heart, and made them plastic; he created, not abstract types, but men and women, charging them with spiritual force; and the result is that Ethan Brand, with his homely garments and heavy shoes, bending over the fiery lime-kiln on the slope of Hoosac, is a figure with all the moral passion, the tragic dignity, of Empedocles of old casting himself despairingly into the crater of Mount Etna.

It is more than fifty years since Hawthorne left the village at the foot of Greylock, never to return. Most of the companions of his sojourn there lie buried in the cone-shaped sand-hills of the crowded cemetery just beyond the Little Tunnel. The Whig Tavern changed hands shortly after his departure; and although Orrin Smith later kept another hostelry by the side of the old coaching road on the crest of Hoosac, that, too, has long since disappeared, and the site is overgrown with alders. But within ten minutes' walk of the Tunnel City may still be seen a gray lime-kiln upon which Hawthorne's eyes have rested, and the intense personal emotion of that long-past year is still vibrant in *Ethan Brand*. The romance-writers of our day have learned to stray far afield in their search for material, and they come back, too often, with such empty hands! The more's the pity, since a factory village, set in a narrow space among New England hills, was once field enough for a Hawthorne.

FISHING WITH A WORM

FISHING WITH A WORM.

"The last fish I caught was with a worm." — IZAAK WALTON.

A DEFECTIVE logic is the born fisherman's portion. He is a pattern of inconsistency. He does the things which he ought not to do, and he leaves undone the things which other people think he ought to do. He observes the wind when he should be sowing, and he regards the clouds, with temptation tugging familiarly at his heartstrings, when he might be grasping the useful sickle. It is a wonder that there is so much health in him. A sorrowing political economist remarked to me in early boyhood, as a jolly red-bearded neighbor, followed by an abnormally fat dog, sauntered past us for his nooning: "That man is the best carpenter in town, but he will leave the most important job whenever he wants to go fishing." I stared at the sinful carpenter, who swung along leisurely in the May sunshine, keeping just ahead of his dog. To leave one's job in order to go fishing! How illogical!

Years bring the reconciling mind. The world grows big enough to include within its scheme both the instructive political economist and the truant mechanic. But that trick of truly logical behavior seems harder to the man than to the child. For example, I climbed up to my den under the eaves last night — a sour, black sea-fog lying all about, and the December sleet crackling against the window-panes — in order to varnish a certain fly-rod. Now rods ought to be put in order in September, when the fishing closes, or else in April, when it opens. To varnish a rod in December proves that one possesses either a dilatory or a childishly anticipatory mind. But before uncorking the varnish bottle, it occurred to me to examine a dog-eared, water-stained fly-book, to guard against the ravages of possible moths. This interlude proved fatal to the varnishing. A half hour went happily by in rearranging the flies. Then, with a fisherman's lack of sequence, as I picked out here and there a plain snell-hook from the gaudy feathered ones, I said to myself with a generous glow at the heart: "Fly-fishing has had enough sacred poets celebrating it already. Is n't there a good deal to be said, after all, for fishing with a worm?"

Could there be a more illogical proceeding? And here follows the treatise, — a Defense of Results, an Apology for Opportunism, — conceived in agreeable procrastination, devoted to the praise of the inconsequential angleworm, and dedicated to a childish memory of a whistling carpenter and his fat dog.

Let us face the worst at the very beginning. It shall be a shameless example of fishing under conditions that make the fly a mockery. Take the Taylor Brook, "between the roads," on the headwaters of the Lamoille. The place is a jungle. The swamp maples and cedars were felled a generation ago, and the tops were trimmed into the brook. The alders and moosewood are higher than your head; on every tiny knoll the fir balsams have gained a footing, and creep down, impenetrable, to the edge of the water. In the open spaces the Joe-Pye weed swarms. In two minutes after leaving the upper road you have scared a mink or a rabbit, and you have probably lost the brook. Listen! It is only a gurgle here, droning along, smooth and dark, under the tangle of cedar-tops and the shadow of the balsams. Follow the sound cautiously. There, beyond the Joe-Pye weed, and between the stump and the cedar-top, is a hand's breadth of black water. Fly-casting is impossible in this maze of dead and living branches. Shorten your line to two feet, or even less, bait your hook with a worm, and drop it gingerly into that gurgling crevice of water. Before it has sunk six inches, if there is not one of those black-backed, orange-bellied, Taylor Brook trout fighting with it, something is wrong with your worm or with you. For the trout are always there, sheltered by the brushwood that makes this half mile of fishing " not worth while." Below the lower road the Taylor Brook becomes uncertain water. For half a mile it yields only fingerlings, for no explainable reason; then there are two miles of clean fishing through the deep woods, where the branches are so high that you can cast a fly again if you like, and there are long pools, where now and then a heavy fish will rise; then comes a final half mile through the alders, where you must wade, knee to waist deep, before you come to the bridge and the river. Glorious fishing is sometimes to be had here, —

FISHING WITH A WORM

especially if you work down the gorge at twilight, casting a white miller until it is too dark to see. But alas, there is a well-worn path along the brook, and often enough there are the very footprints of the " fellow ahead of you," signs as disheartening to the fisherman as ever were the footprints on the sand to Robinson Crusoe.

But " between the roads " it is " too much trouble to fish ; " and there lies the salvation of the humble fisherman who disdains not to use the crawling worm, nor, for that matter, to crawl himself, if need be, in order to sneak under the boughs of some overhanging cedar that casts a perpetual shadow upon the sleepy brook. Lying here at full length, with no elbow-room to manage the rod, you must occasionally even unjoint your tip, and fish with that, using but a dozen inches of line, and not letting so much as your eyebrows show above the bank. Is it a becoming attitude for a middle-aged citizen of the world ? That depends upon how the fish are biting. Holing a put looks rather ridiculous also, to the mere observer, but it requires, like brook-fishing with a tip only, a very delicate wrist, perfect tactile sense, and a fine disregard of appearances.

There are some fishermen who always fish as if they were being photographed. The Taylor Brook " between the roads " is not for them. To fish it at all is back-breaking, trouser-tearing work; to see it thoroughly fished is to learn new lessons in the art of angling. To watch R., for example, steadily filling his six-pound creel from that unlikely stream, is like watching Sargent paint a portrait. R. weighs two hundred and ten. Twenty years ago he was a famous amateur pitcher, and among his present avocations are violin playing, which is good for the wrist, taxidermy, which is good for the eye, and shooting woodcock, which before the days of the new Nature Study used to be thought good for the whole man. R. began as a fly-fisherman, but by dint of passing his summers near brooks where fly-fishing is impossible, he has become a stout-hearted apologist for the worm. His apparatus is most singular. It consists of a very long, cheap rod, stout enough to smash through bushes, and with the stiffest tip obtainable. The lower end of the butt, below the reel, fits into the socket of a huge extra butt of bamboo, which R. carries unconcernedly. To reach a distant hole, or to fish the lower end of a ripple, R. simply locks his reel, slips on the extra butt, and there is a fourteen-foot rod ready for action. He fishes with a line unbelievably short, and a Kendal hook far too big; and when a trout jumps for that hook, R. wastes no time in manœuvring for position. The unlucky fish is simply " derricked," — to borrow a word from Theodore, most saturnine and profane of Moosehead guides.

" Shall I play him awhile? " shouted an excited sportsman to Theodore, after hooking his first big trout.

"——— no! "growled Theodore in disgust. "Just derrick him right into the canoe! " A heroic method, surely; though it once cost me the best square-tail I ever hooked, for Theodore had forgotten the landing-net, and the gut broke in his fingers as he tried to swing the fish aboard. But with these lively quarter-pounders of the Taylor Brook, derricking is a safer procedure. Indeed, I have sat dejectedly on the far end of a log, after fishing the hole under it in vain, and seen the mighty R. wade downstream close behind me, adjust that comical extra butt, and jerk a couple of half-pound trout from under the very log on which I was sitting. His device on this occasion, as I well remember, was to pass his hook but once through the middle of a big worm, let the worm sink to the bottom, and crawl along it at his leisure. The trout could not resist.

Once, and once only, have I come near equaling R.'s record, and the way he beat me then is the justification for a whole philosophy of worm-fishing. We were on this very Taylor Brook, and at five in the afternoon both baskets were two thirds full. By count I had just one more fish than he. It was raining hard. " You fish down through the alders," said R. magnanimously. " I'll cut across and wait for you at the sawmill. I don't want to get any wetter, on account of my rheumatism."

This was rather barefaced kindness, — for whose rheumatism was ever the worse for another hour's fishing? But I weakly accepted it. I coveted three or four good trout to top off with, — that was all. So I tied on a couple of flies, and began to fish the alders, wading waist deep in the rapidly rising water, down the long green tunnel under the curving boughs. The brook fairly smoked with the rain, by this time, but

FISHING WITH A WORM

when did one fail to get at least three or four trout out of this best half mile of the lower brook? Yet I had no luck. I tried one fly after another, and then, as a forlorn hope, — though it sometimes has a magic of its own,— I combined a brown hackle for the tail fly with a twisting worm on the dropper. Not a rise! I thought of R. sitting patiently in the saw mill, and I fished more conscientiously than ever.

> "Venture as warily, use the same skill,
> Do your best, whether winning or losing it,
> If you choose to play ! — is my principle."

Even those lines, which by some subtle telepathy of the trout brook murmur themselves over and over to me in the waning hours of an unlucky day, brought now no consolation. There was simply not one fish to be had, to any fly in the book, out of that long, drenching, darkening tunnel. At last I climbed out of the brook, by the bridge. R. was sitting on the fence, his neck and ears carefully turtled under his coat collar, the smoke rising and the rain dripping from the inverted bowl of his pipe. He did not seem to be worrying about his rheumatism.

"What luck?" he asked.

"None at all," I answered morosely. "Sorry to keep you waiting."

"That's all right," remarked R. "What do you think I've been doing? I've been fishing out of the saw-mill window just to kill time. There was a patch of floating sawdust there, — kind of unlikely place for trout, anyway, — but I thought I'd put on a worm and let him crawl around a little." He opened his creel as he spoke.

"But I did n't look for a pair of 'em," he added. And there, on top of his smaller fish, were as pretty a pair of three-quarter-pound brook trout as were ever basketed.

"I'm afraid you got pretty wet," said R. kindly.

"I don't mind that," I replied. And I did n't. What I minded was the thought of an hour's vain wading in that roaring stream, whipping it with fly after fly, while R., the foreordained fisherman, was sitting comfortably in a sawmill, and derricking that pair of three-quarter-pounders in through the window! I had ventured more warily than he, and used, if not the same skill, at least the best skill at my command. My conscience was clear, but so was his; and he had had the drier skin and the greater magnanimity and the biggest fish besides. There is much to be said, in a world like ours, for taking the world as you find it and for fishing with a worm.

One's memories of such fishing, however agreeable they may be, are not to be identified with a defense of the practice. Yet, after all, the most effective defense of worm-fishing is the concrete recollection of some brook that could be fished best or only in that way, or the image of a particular trout that yielded to the temptation of an angleworm after you had flicked fly after fly over him in vain. Indeed, half the zest of brook fishing is in your campaign for "individuals," — as the Salvation Army workers say, — not merely for a basketful of fish *qua* fish, but for a series of individual trout which your instinct tells you ought to lurk under that log or be hovering in that ripple. How to get him, by some sportsmanlike process, is the question. If he will rise to some fly in your book, few fishermen will deny that the fly is the more pleasurable weapon. Dainty, luring, beautiful toy, light as thistle-down, falling where you will it to fall, holding when the leader tightens and sings like the string of a violin, the artificial fly represents the poetry of angling. Given the gleam of early morning on some wide water, a heavy trout breaking the surface as he curves and plunges, with the fly holding well, with the right sort of rod in your fingers, and the right man in the other end of the canoe, and you perceive how easy is that Emersonian trick of making the pomp of emperors ridiculous.

But angling's honest prose, as represented by the lowly worm, has also its exalted moments. "The last fish I caught was with a worm," says the honest Walton, and so say I. It was the last evening of last August. The dusk was settling deep upon a tiny meadow, scarcely ten rods from end to end. The rank bog grass, already drenched with dew, bent over the narrow, deep little brook so closely that it could not be fished except with a double-shotted, baited hook, dropped delicately between the heads of the long grasses. Underneath this canopy the trout were feeding, taking the hook with a straight downward tug, as they made for the hidden bank. It was already twilight when I began, and before I reached the black belt of woods that separated the meadow from the lake, the swift darkness of the North Country made it impossible to see the hook. A short half hour's fishing only, and behold nearly twenty good trout derricked into a basket until then sadly empty. Your rigorous fly-fisherman would have passed that grass-hidden brook in disdain, but it proved a treasure for the humble.

Here, indeed, there was no question of individually-minded fish, but simply a neglected brook, full of trout which could be reached with the baited hook only. In more open brook-fishing it is always a fascinating problem to decide how to fish a favorite pool or ripple, for much depends upon the hour of the day, the light, the height of water, the precise period of the spring or summer. But after one has decided upon the best theoretical procedure, how often the stupid trout prefers some other plan! And when you have missed a fish that you counted upon landing, what solid satisfaction is still possible for you, if you are philosopher enough to sit down then and there, eat your lunch, smoke a meditative pipe, and devise a new campaign against that particular fish! To get another rise from him after lunch is a triumph of diplomacy; to land him is nothing short of statesmanship. For sometimes he will jump furiously at a fly, for very devilishness, without ever meaning to take it, and then, wearying suddenly of his gymnastics, he will snatch sulkily at a grasshopper, beetle, or worm. Trout feed upon an extraordinary variety of crawling things, as all fishermen know who practice the useful habit of opening the first two or three fish they catch, to see what food is that day the favorite. But here, as elsewhere in this world, the best things lie nearest, and there is no bait so killing, week in and week out, as your plain garden or golf-green angleworm.

Walton's list of possible worms is impressive, and his directions for placing them upon the hook have the placid completeness that belonged to his character. Yet in such matters a little nonconformity may be encouraged. No two men or boys dig bait in quite the same way, though all share, no doubt, the singular elation which gilds that grimy occupation with the spirit of romance. The mind is really occupied, not with the wriggling red creatures in the lumps of earth, but with the stout fish which each worm may capture, just as a saint might rejoice in the squalor of this world as a preparation for the glories of the world to come. Nor do any two experienced fishermen hold quite the same theory as to the best mode of baiting the hook. There are a hundred ways, each of them good. As to the best hook for worm-fishing, you will find dicta in every catalogue of fishing tackle, but size and shape and tempering are qualities that should vary with the brook, the season, and the fisherman. Should one use a three-foot leader, or none at all? Whose rods are best for bait-fishing, granted that all of them should be stiff enough in the tip to lift a good fish by dead strain from a tangle of brush or logs? Such questions, like those pertaining to the boots or coat which one should wear, the style of bait-box one should carry, or the brand of tobacco best suited for smoking in the wind, are topics for unending discussion among the serious minded around the camp-fire. Much edification is in them, and yet they are but prudential maxims after all. They are mere moralities of the Franklin or Chesterfield variety, counsels of worldly wisdom, but they leave the soul untouched. A man may have them at his finger's ends and be no better fisherman at bottom; or he may, like R., ignore most of the admitted rules and come home with a full basket. It is a sufficient defense of fishing with a worm to pronounce the truism that no man is a *complete* angler until he has mastered all the modes of angling. Lovely streams, lonely and enticing, but impossible to fish with a fly, await the fisherman who is not too proud to use, with a man's skill, the same unpretentious tackle which he began with as a boy.

But ah, to fish with a worm, and then not catch your fish! To fail with a fly is no disgrace: your art may have been impeccable, your patience faultless to the end. But the philosophy of worm-fishing is that of Results, of having something tangible in your basket when the day's work is done. It is a plea for Compromise, for cutting the coat according to the cloth, for taking the world as it actually is. The fly-fisherman is a natural Foe of Compromise. He throws to the trout a certain kind of lure; an they will take it, so; if not, adieu. He knows no middle path.

> "This high man, aiming at a million,
>   Misses an unit."

FISHING WITH A WORM

The raptures and the tragedies of consistency are his. He is a scorner of the ground. All honor to him! When he comes back at nightfall and says happily, "I have never cast a line more perfectly than I have to-day," it is almost indecent to peek into his creel. It is like rating Colonel Newcome by his bank account.

But the worm-fisherman is no such proud and isolated soul. He is a "low man" rather than a high one; he honestly cares what his friends will think when they look into his basket to see what he has to show for his day's sport. He watches the Foe of Compromise men go stumbling forward and superbly falling, while he, with less inflexible courage, manages to keep his feet. He wants to score, and not merely to give a pretty exhibition of base-running. At the Harvard-Yale football game of 1903 the Harvard team showed superior strength in rushing the ball; they carried it almost to the Yale goal line repeatedly, but they could not, for some reason, take it over. In the instant of absolute need, the Yale line held, and when the Yale team had to score in order to win, they scored. As the crowd streamed out of the Stadium, a veteran Harvard alumnus said: "This news will cause great sorrow in one home I know of, until they learn by to-morrow's papers that the Harvard team *acquitted itself creditably.*" Exactly. Given one team bent upon acquitting itself creditably, and another team determined to win, which will be victorious? The stay-at-homes on the Yale campus that day were not curious to know whether their team was acquitting itself creditably, but whether it was winning the game. Every other question than that was to those young Philistines merely a fine-spun irrelevance. They took the Cash and let the Credit go.

There is much to be said, no doubt, for the Harvard veteran's point of view. The proper kind of credit may be a better asset for eleven boys than any championship; and to fish a bit of water consistently and skillfully, with your best flies and in your best manner, is perhaps achievement enough. So says the Foe of Compromise, at least. But the Yale spirit will be prying into the basket in search of fish; it prefers concrete results. If all men are by nature either Platonists or Aristotelians, fly-fishermen or worm-fishermen, how difficult it is for us to do one another justice! Differing in mind, in aim and method, how shall we say infallibly that this man or that is wrong? To fail with Plato for companion may be better than to succeed with Aristotle. But one thing is perfectly clear: there is no warrant for Compromise but in Success. Use a worm if you will, but you must have fish to show for it, if you would escape the finger of scorn. If you find yourself camping by an unknown brook, and are deputed to catch the necessary trout for breakfast, it is wiser to choose the surest bait. The crackle of the fish in the frying-pan will atone for any theoretical defect in your method. But to choose the surest bait, and then to bring back no fish, is unforgivable. Forsake Plato if you must, — but you may do so only at the price of justifying yourself in the terms of Aristotelian arithmetic. The college president who abandoned his college in order to run a cotton mill was free to make his own choice of a calling; but he was never pardoned for bankrupting the mill. If one is bound to be a low man rather than an impractical idealist, he should at least make sure of his vulgar success.

Is all this but a disguised defense of pot-hunting? No. There is no possible defense of pot-hunting, whether it be upon a trout brook or in the stock market. Against fish or men, one should play the game fairly. Yet for that matter some of the most skillful fly-fishermen I have known were pot-hunters at heart, and some of the most prosaic-looking merchants were idealists compared to whom Shelley was but a dreaming boy. All depends upon the spirit with which one makes his venture. I recall a boy of five who gravely watched his father tramp off after rabbits, — gun on shoulder and beagle in leash. Thereupon he shouldered a wooden sword, and dragging his reluctant black kitten by a string, sallied forth upon the dusty Vermont road " to get a lion for breakfast." That is the true sporting temper! Let there be but a fine idealism in the quest, and the particular object is unessential. "A true fisherman's happiness," says Mr. Cleveland, "is not dependent upon his luck." It depends upon his heart.

No doubt all amateur fishing is but "play," — as the psychologists soberly term it: not a necessary, but a freely assumed activity, born of surplusage of vitality. Nobody, not even a carpenter wearied of his job, has to go fishing unless he wants to. He may indeed find himself breakfastless in camp, and obliged to betake himself to the brook, — but then he need not have gone into the woods at all. Yet if he does decide to fish, let him

> " Venture as warily, use the same skill,
> Do his best, . . . "

whatever variety of tackle he may choose. He can be a whole-souled sportsman with the poorest equipment, or a mean " trout-hog " with the most elaborate.

Only, in the name of gentle Izaak himself, let him be a *complete* angler; and let the man be a passionate amateur of all the arts of life, despising none of them, and using all of them for his soul's good and for the joy of his fellows. If he be, so to speak, but a worm-fisherman, — a follower of humble occupations, and pledged to unromantic duties, — let him still thrill with the pleasures of the true sportsman. To make the most of dull hours, to make the best of dull people, to like a poor jest better than none, to wear the threadbare coat like a gentleman, to be outvoted with a smile, to hitch your wagon to the old horse if no star is handy, — this is the wholesome philosophy taught by fishing with a worm. The fun of it depends upon the heart. There may be as much zest in saving as in spending, in working for small wages as for great, in avoiding the snapshots of publicity as in being invariably first "among those present." But a man should be honest. If he catches most of his fish with a worm, secures the larger portion of his success by commonplace industry, let him glory in it, for this, too, is part of the great game. Yet he ought not in that case to pose as a fly-fisherman only, — to carry himself as one aware of the immortalizing camera, — to pretend that life is easy, if one but knows how to drop a fly into the right ripple. For life is not easy, after all is said. It is a long brook to fish, and it needs a stout heart and a wise patience. All the flies there are in the book, and all the bait that can be carried in the box, are likely to be needed ere the day is over. But, like the Psalmist's "river of God," this brook is "full of water," and there is plenty of good fishing to be had in it if one is neither afraid nor ashamed of fishing sometimes with a worm.